FROM PAUPERS

TO iPADS®

Tony Berry is a journalist, editor and author who has worked on newspapers, journals and magazines in the UK and Australia, where he emigrated several decades ago. He recently made a spur of the moment decision to return to the UK and set up base in Cornwall while researching his family history. He continues to edit fiction and non-fiction for clients in Australia and the UK and was recently appointed editor of the Journal of the Cornwall Family History Society. He devotes much of his spare time to running and for several years has been recognised as an elite competitor in masters athletics at national and international level for distances from 10km to the full marathon. His first two crime novels were short-listed for the New South Wales Genre Fiction Award and the third is close to completion.

Also by Tony Berry

The Bromo Perkins Crime Series

Done Deal

Washed Up

FROM PAUPERS

TO iPADS®

A journey through

seven generations

by

TONY BERRY

FastPrint Publishing
www.fast-print.net/store.php

From Paupers to iPads
Copyright © Tony Berry 2011

All rights reserved

No part of this book may be reproduced in any form by photocopying or any electronic or mechanical means, including information storage or retrieval systems, without permission in writing from both the copyright owner and the publisher of the book.

Cover design © 2011 by Lynne Tasker

ISBN 978-178035-217-6

Published 2011 by
FASTPRINT PUBLISHING
Peterborough, England.

Dedicated to all my ancestors and forebears in honour of the hard lives so many of them endured and with apologies for any distortions, inaccuracies or aspersions that may have been unwittingly and unintentionally cast upon them in creating this admittedly fanciful story of their lives. All corrections, amendments and adjustments will be gratefully received and acknowledged. Deepest thanks, too, to the many co-researchers, family historians and hitherto unknown relatives who have provided help and information – and to the staunchest helper and supporter of them all, my hitherto unknown cousin and now partner Lynne Tasker, without whose dogged digging, eye for detail and endless enthusiasm and encouragement much of this would not have been possible.

Where we have come from is as important as where we are headed

FOREWORD

THERE is a widely-held belief that journalists abide by a rule that states 'never let the facts spoil a good story'. Having worked as a newspaper scribe for more than fifty years, it is an allegation I strongly deny.

Facts are paramount. Strenuous efforts are always made to verify them – despite the obstacles provided by those who prefer their own distorted version of events. It is in the handling of the facts where things so often go awry, resulting in the slurs cast against well-intentioned journos. The hows, whys and wherefores behind the facts are where interpretation so often varies.

The following work is one that proves facts can be used in whatever way the writer chooses and I cheerfully confess to having played fast and loose with the information at hand.

The facts are rock solid; dates, names and places have all been researched and documented. However, as with all data, it is the events surrounding these facts that are open to interpretation.

Like most family researchers I came too late to my task. I began delving into the past long after my ancestors had passed on. All that remain are dates and names and often questionable records. The voices that could relate stories of family life, explain events and justify decisions fell silent decades ago.

And so it was left to me to weave my own stories; to embroider the facts in order to enliven what would otherwise be a mundane set of names and dates. Imagined conversations, decisions and actions have been attached to real people to show how our ancestors lived – and give my daughter and my grandsons a link into their past.

It has been a long and enthralling journey helped by a global confection of many willing co-researchers, distant kinfolk and archivists and, above all, by my constant companion and newfound cousin, Lynne Tasker, who has painstakingly assisted in my research and corrected my many errors.

TONY BERRY,
Cornwall, November 2011

EMAILS CAN BE RELATIVE

IT was a message out of the blue. Emails are like that; they are disturbingly instant, not only in the way they drop unannounced into a computer's Inbox but also in the way they confront the recipient. There is no puzzling over the sender's identity as there is with an unexpected letter received by snail mail. There is no examining the postmark, no pondering the handwriting, wondering about the sender and the contents. It's there: on your desktop and in your face.

Thus did cousin Lynne reveal what was to me her hitherto unknown existence. And thus, too, began a journey that both of us had only vaguely considered and which, until she pressed the send button, was destined to be travelled alone. Both had been tracing our family histories – she in Cornwall, in England's wild southwest, and me in the inner suburbs of Melbourne, Australia's heartland of culture and caffeine.

Her probing, much deeper and far more efficient than mine, had taken her back to the 1840s when one of her line had hitched up with one of my line. The knots were tied and, three generations later, we were entwined as cousins. And in a most delightful way, as events somewhat rapidly proved.

Lynne's was not the only contact received via cyberspace. Other previously unheard-of relatives emerged in Bournemouth, Essex, Swindon and close to the grandparental home in Yorkshire. But she was by far the most persistent and most positive. A shared enthusiasm for ancestral detection was evident very early on. Even better, her emails were literate and witty. They showed a quirky sense of humour based on a love of words and language. The rapport was as instant as hot water and Nescafe, and much more to my liking than that dubious brew.

The exchange of emails and information became much more frequent, confirming the relationship and throwing up even more links. Lynne's home was but a few kilometres from that of my sister and at one stage they had lived only a few houses apart yet totally unaware of their ancestral ties. Even stranger still, it eventually emerged that in much earlier times our two families had lived in similar close proximity as neighbours and workmates in Pembrokeshire in the southwest corner of Wales.

Within weeks email contact was dispensed with in favour of instantaneous exchanges through the wonder of Skype – at first via text and then warily revealing ourselves by video. Genealogy had never been so much fun, nor so instantaneous. Already, thanks to the internet, research that would have been a lengthy and painstaking task only a few years ago now took only moments. Through this contact across the globe, our research could be debated and analysed at the press of a button. It was no longer detached and impersonal and we ceased working in isolation, unable to check facts or verify connections.

Four months after Lynne's first email a vague thought of some day walking the streets of my forebears had blossomed into an undeniable urge. As every new detail was uncovered and each personal trait revealed there was an exciting inevitability about our relationship. And so began an intensely personal odyssey that took me way beyond the mere compilation of a mundane family tree with its clusters of boxes linking names across the generations. Family research took on a whole new meaning and among my kith and kin the phrase became a euphemism for something other than delving into dusty archives.

My journey took me from Melbourne via London to mystical Cornwall, in England's far southwest, and Lynne's home in the cathedral city of Truro. From there were travelled together to the hilly streets of ancient Haverfordwest in the westernmost Wales. There, within the solid walls of the ruined castle that looms over the town, we pored over parish records, workhouse registers, archives, manuscripts and maps helped by a friendly staff with a seemingly inexhaustible knowledge of the region's past.

One lesson was soon learnt: family researchers need to be precise in their enquiries. It is essential to go armed with definite questions. To enter the Public Records Office and state you are researching the Smith family will get you nowhere in a long time. However, quite the opposite is achieved by saying you are trying to trace the marriage of John Smith from such and such a parish around about 1815. Old handwritten documents will be speedily produced and you will be directed where next to look in your research. Our two mornings in Haverfordwest Castle produced marriage details, two wills made in the 1780s, details of family donations to a village school, an invaluable map and the revelation of a coroner's report into a family member's death of which we had no previous knowledge. This latter document provided evidence that the family had lived at an address in Pembroke Dock some thirty years earlier than we had previously thought. We were off and running like foxhounds finding a new scent. There were streets to walk, houses to find and mysteries to solve.

Chief among the latter was the whereabouts of the village of Coombs where my great-great-grandparents once lived. Yet, although there is no doubt Coombs existed way back in the medieval era, at some time over the past hundred years or so it seems to have been wiped off the map. It definitely existed in 1851 when William John Berry, his wife Ann and their ten children were recorded in the census as living 'in the last house in the village of Coombs'.

It was a community within the parish of Steynton, a strip of land six miles from north to south and no more than two miles from east to west yet, in the 1830s, home to some 3000 people. Many of these, however, would have lived in the borough of Milford, the seaport and market town on the shores of Milford Haven, which formed the parish's southern boundary.

A tidal inlet, the Hubbertson Pill, provided access to Coombs at high tide for small craft. Although largely agricultural, the parish also contained deposits of culm that were extracted at a mine on Lord Kensington's estate and provided the district's needs for cheap fuel.

Coombs was still there in 1880, according to a map of Pembrokeshire produced by the archivists beavering away in the castle's Public Record Office. But not even their willing determination could produce any references more recent than that. A painstaking trawl through the archives eventually dashed all hopes of retracing my forebears' footsteps among the farmhouses and cottages of Coombs. Extensive searches proved the village once existed along the creeks flowing inland from the vast waterway that is now Milford harbour. Now it is no more: vanished, gone without a trace. Neither the intensely detailed Ordnance Survey maps nor the usually reliable Google maps recognised its existence.

Then, two days into a tour of the area, we had a Eureka moment. In a tourist guide to Milford Haven, picked up as we rifled through a rack of brochures in the hotel foyer, was that elusive name: Coombs – surely its only inclusion on a modern map … and precisely where I believed it should have been. It was simply a word in an otherwise blank space as if the artist felt the need to put something there. All roads may very well lead to Rome, but we found none that led to Coombs.

As testimony to the past there is, however, the Coombs Road that turns off the main route from the medieval community of Steynton (where my folks later lived) to the modern harbour port of Milford Haven that later subsumed it. Little more than a country lane, Coombs Road plunges and twists its way down to the muddy and tidal Pill Creek before hair-pinning up the other side to Venn Farm and Castle Hall, which were both prominent on maps of John Berry's time. A minor industrial estate now stands where a vineyard once struggled for existence in a climate hardly conducive to viticulture. A quarry and lime kilns are now also nothing more than landmarks on old maps.

A few clicks of the milometer past Venn Farm we noticed one of those ubiquitous walking man signs indicating a footpath heading off to the left in the direction of the woods and Pill Creek. To seekers of the past, however, this was no ordinary sign. It was a true sign in the fullest, almost biblical, sense; a pointer to our holy grail.

We followed the rough narrow trail between fenced-off farm meadows, slowly descending towards the thickly wooded slopes bordering the creek. On either side were the remnants of solidly thick old stone walls barely discernable beneath masses of brambles and undergrowth. Someone once lived here.

The final few metres sloped steeply down then broadened out to a gravelly creek bed. A lively stream flowed down from dense woods on our right, rippling over a ford and on into the creek. The view to our left opened out, the creek widening into a broad expanse of mudflats and minor streams rimmed by wooded hillsides. I was home! This was where my direct ancestors lived; the wellspring and source of the many Berrys that followed.

Somewhere up to the right, among the tree-covered slopes and overlooking the bend in the creek, was as far back as I could trace my existence. A light breeze ruffled the branches. A weak September sun dappled the water. It was such a peaceful and almost hidden corner of this troubled and angry world. We stood there in total silence. Emotions dictated this was not the time for words.

Little was said on the walk back to Coombs Road and the next stage of the journey – a long and winding trail that eventually resulted in the pages that follow.

MARKING TIME

MY great-grandparents signed their wedding certificate by making their mark. They were too illiterate to write their own names. Already, as they enter their teenage years, my two grandsons, like so many of their peers, are highly computer literate. They are masters of text messaging and the iPad, and are able to converse intelligently on a vast array of complex topics.

The boys have grown used to my technical ineptitude. They know whenever I stay over they will have to help me operate the finger-touch stove top, the video player, the microwave oven and even the coffee machine – all marvels of technology that somehow cause me endless trouble and bafflement.

To Logan and Liam such items are but tools of modern life. As are the laptop computers they use with ease and the CDs and DVDs they nonchalantly flip into video players. More recently there arrived the tantalising Wii, a piddling device that sadly encourages us to play lifelike golf, tennis and tenpin bowling without leaving the lounge room or truly exercising our bodies.

My grandfather would never have imagined the existence of such devices. Nor, when he was the age Liam and Logan are now, would he even have dreamed of sitting as they frequently do in a metal tube that soars into the sky and transports them across the globe in less than a day.

Gramp's familiarity with machines that could fly came late in life by way of the Spitfires and Messerschmitts that fought the Battle of Britain overhead while he ran for shelter from the German bombs raining down on the dockyard where he worked.

To him, aircraft were machines of war, not the pleasure craft that took Liam and Logan to the Kennedy Space Centre in the USA, where they sampled the life of the astronauts and experienced the thrill of space travel with everything but the actual blast-off.

As my grandsons gaze into the stratosphere and beyond, I look back and marvel at how far our humble line has come in a mere two hundred and fifty years – and at the changes my ancestors experienced along the way. Perhaps there is nothing remarkable in my family's generational contrasts; after all, the past two centuries have seen the most rapid changes in the world's history and the pace of change continues to accelerate daily.

However, in shifting my focus from the general to the personal, I found it fascinating to unravel my family's steady progress from the lower levels of a downtrodden British working class to their present position as relatively prosperous and respected participants in so many aspects of society that were inaccessible to my ancestors.

As my technically aware and highly literate grandsons help me cope with the intricacies of infrared cooking, I can't help but ponder the journey the family has made from the Welsh shipyards and Yorkshire mills of the 1830s to the 'all mod-cons' of a four-hectare Australian bush retreat at the start of the twenty-first century.

It's a journey I had to retrace and one which Logan and Liam may also one day take. They might even discover even more surprises and secrets than those that came my way. Where we have come from is as important as where we are headed.

DREAMS OF FRENCH GRANDEUR

FAMILY historians are dreamers and eternal optimists. They trawl through parish records, censuses and libraries, living with the hope of discovering their roots go back to some notable, a member of the landed gentry or even to undiscovered fortunes. We sit on our suburban blocks spurred on by the fantasy that the ancestral home is a chateau in the Loire or a grand mansion nestled in hectares of English woodland.

My own grandiose dream was that the Berry family tree was firmly grounded in rich French soil and that our first steps on to English turf were a result of the Norman invasion. There were fanciful visions of a distant and noble patriarch riding forth with banners waving at the head of a troop of loyal supporters. And why not? The family name lives on in an ancient region of central France that embraces the great chateaux of Loire Valley and such noble cities as Bourges, Chartres, Tours and Joan of Arc's fateful Orleans.

The strongest of Gaul's Celtic tribes, the Bituriges Cubi, occupied Berry around 600 BC. It later became part of the Roman province of Aquitania Prima, was passed to the Franks in the sixth century and then was ruled by a line of hereditary nobles until 1200, when the French kings gained control and created the title Duke of Berry.

The first holder of the title, in 1360, was John, third son of King John II. Although he was a mediocre and greedy warlord, John of Berry was a notable patron who enjoyed art, music, hunting and good food. He sounds like a man after my own heart; an excellent candidate for ancestor status. He collected precious manuscripts, jewels, enamels, tapestries, birds and exotic animals and sponsored the best artists.

Today, he is mostly known for commissioning (between 1413 and 1416) the wonderful illuminated book called *Les Très Riches Heures du Duc de Berry*, now preserved in the Condé Museum in Chantilly and a copy of which has long been prominent on my own bookshelves.

It was when I stumbled across these incredibly beautiful illustrated manuscripts that my fanciful belief in cultured French royal ancestors first started to germinate. Oh that our heritage could lay claim to an association with this glorious treasure of the Middle Ages – and with the passionate patron who made it possible.

Sadly, John's spending on his art collection severely taxed his estates and he was deeply in debt when he died in Paris in 1416. As there was no surviving male issue the title was recreated for his great-nephew, the Dauphin John, Duke of Touraine, eldest son of King Charles VI, who died shortly afterwards. Various other lesser royals (including two Margarets) were handed the title over the following centuries until it came to an abrupt end with Duke Charles Ferdinand's assassination in 1820.

So, after the spendthrift glory days of Duke John – a name much used throughout our family tree – the French clan that gave birth to the Berry name did little of merit or note and slowly drifted into oblivion. I have tried to attain glory by association on tours through the bucolic Berry countryside during which I visited the glorious Chartres Cathedral and even stayed a couple of memorable nights at Château de Chambord and Château de Chenonceaux where, no doubt, the Berrys once rested and roistered.

Unfortunately, try as I might and willing so hard for it to be true, not one of them can be linked to our very much more humble line of Berrys.

This same rampant optimism also had me exploring the magnificent Manorbier Castle – an arrow's flight from my ancestral roots in south Wales. It was built by the du Barri family in Norman times when the spelling of names took numerous variations. It was a false but memorable trail along which the only vague ancestral link was via the castle's network of tunnel. There were once used by the numerous smugglers who were pursued along the Pembrokeshire coast by much-scorned tidewaiters and Customs officers, one of whom was my great-great-grandfather William Berry.

But it's good to dream and that, as every family historian soon discovers, is much of what genealogy is all about and is the spur that urges us ancestor-seekers on.

QUESTIONS WE FORGET TO ASK

AH regrets, I have a few (but only a few and more of those much later) … and one of the strongest is that I never delved into my parents' past, or that of their parents. As I started out on the tortuous road known as family history I soon began wondering, like so many others before me, why kids don't think of asking questions until it's far too late.

It is a lesson to be noted and acted upon by anyone making an attempt to answer that intriguing riddle of 'Who am I?'

My research turned what had hitherto been a mundane past into a trail of inquests, workplace deaths, puzzling bequests, unknown migrations and the moving discovery of a great-uncle's grave in Flanders fields. Throw in a romance that came right out of left field and you have the stuff of historical novels – my very own readymade pot-boiler lurking in the foliage of the family tree.

In trying to trace my heritage, and hopefully leave something of interest and value to future generations, I realised the only reason I knew far too little of my family's history was because of my own negligence. As a lifelong journalist, I am steeped in the basics of who, what, why, when and how and yet never once applied these words to my parents and those that came before.

About all I knew was that on the maternal side Gramp came from Dewsbury in Yorkshire and Nan from Battle in Sussex, aptly named for the brief struggle that occurred nearby when William the Conqueror decided he would add a bit of England to his French real estate holdings.

It's also little more than a fast messenger's ride from the French estates where the flamboyant Duc du Berry once held sway and created those famously incredible illuminated manuscripts that I falsely dreamed might be a family heirloom.

But how did these people from the opposite ends of the country come together in an era when ordinary folk looked upon such journeys as akin to flying to the moon? What brought a man from a tight-knit community among the mines and mills of the industrial north to the gentler lands of the Sussex Weald and to a career-changing job in the shipyards of the Medway?

I cannot recall talk of brothers and sisters, of which I now know they both had several, or of their parents. And I can only vaguely picture their presence in my life when we lived in the Medway town of Gillingham in that tense and nervy period before war eventually broke out.

Memories of those days are dim, stimulated mostly by a few yellowing photographs and keywords such as Barnsole Road, the Lines (an open space of old fortifications linking Gillingham with Chatham) and Paddy (or 'Pad Pad'), the loyal family dog. And maybe such recollections are distorted by an overlay of later images from when we returned to lodge with Nan and Gramp once peace was declared.

Even the date of our post-war return from Lancashire – where Dad had the good fortune to be posted to do Customs duty on the wharves of Fleetwood, away from the worst of the air raids – is hazy and unable to be confirmed. Parents and grandparents have all passed on and I never thought to ask in all the succeeding years.

The chronology is helped by clinging to a mental image of attending a VE (Victory in Europe) street party in Charter Street – or maybe I am simply recalling familiar scenes of such events and putting myself in a picture where I never was. But it was definitely post-war when I was clutched by Gramp from beneath the fanatical crush at Priestley Road stadium when the barriers on the terraces collapsed as 'the Gills' fought their way into the next round of the FA Cup.

That memory remains as terrifyingly strong as ever. Short, stubby Gramp in his eternal workman's cloth hat, muscled arms wrapped around me, thrusting pugnaciously forward towards the pitch like some scrum half, ball gathered to his chest, torpedoing his way to the touch line.

It was those same sturdy arms, daily exercised with a pair of dumbbells, which would unbuckle the thick belt from around his waist and thrash it down on my backside as punishment for some childish misdemeanour or brattish behaviour. Six of the best, whether meted out in the lounge room or by the headmaster's cane at school, certainly made one think twice before next stepping over well-defined lines.

It seems like harsh justice in today's over-protective world. But the beltings and canings were never done in anger and only after due consideration of the offence and a chance for the miscreant to state his case. You knew the rules. You knew the punishment. There were no idle threats that could be easily ignored. Such was the world from which Gramp, Herbert Newsome, was descended.

MILLWORKERS AND MINERS

DUMPING ON THE PAST

ETERNAL optimism has to be the unwavering philosophy of the dedicated family historian. This is your shockproof shield against the inevitable disappointments waiting on the long road ahead. Imagine, for example, the letdown of having the birthplace of your forefathers described as 'a dump'. Not by some peeved outsider, but by those who live there today. And with depressing frequency, too. Plus unswerving conviction.

Such was my experience with a long-awaited visit to the old Yorkshire town of Dewsbury, home of my mother's side of the family since at least the mid-1700s.

Historians write of it as a town of influence and importance far beyond the Yorkshire borders, or even those of England. It was dour and dependable, as were the people who lived there: proud and hardworking, as solid as the many massive buildings erected to house industry, commerce and the more affluent citizens.

My hope was to capture some vestige of those glory days when Dewsbury's mills were at the centre of the world woollen trade. Perhaps to walk among the looms at a preserved and reconstructed mill; to tread the narrow streets of the back-to-backs – the cramped rows of houses the mill owners built to rent to their workers.

But it was not to be. Sadly, Dewsbury has obliterated its past and seems to care little for its history. It is, as locals frequently offered, a dump: a terminal case gasping to stay alive. Pedestrian malls and bright street furniture scattered around the desolate town centre indicate attempts at civic CPR. But they are overpowered by empty shop fronts, boarded–up windows and a general air of decay and desolation.

And so I ruefully accepted the consensus: a large clump of my family tree is firmly rooted in a dump.

....

Snow swept in off the moors as we drove the last few kilometres towards Dewsbury. It was bleak, cold and wet – somehow in tune with my diminishing expectations of what awaited me.

That morning's newspapers carried the details of the arrest of a Dewsbury woman charged with the murder of her three-year-old daughter. It was the latest in a continuing line of such events in a town that had somehow become used to violence, dysfunction and abuse.

It was to the courtroom of Dewsbury Town Hall that Peter Sutcliffe, the infamous Yorkshire Ripper, was taken after questioning at Dewsbury Police Station to be formally charged in January 1981.

In June 2005, a girl of 12 was charged with grievous bodily harm following what was reported as the attempted hanging of a five year old boy. Mohammad Sidique Khan, the ringleader of the group responsible for the July 2005 London bombings, was discovered to have been living in Lees Holm, Dewsbury. The list of the town's heinous happenings is never ending.

Maps of 1905 and 1847 show line after line of minuscule houses covering the hill alongside the Huddersfield Road, a couple of kilometres from the heart of Dewsbury. On the other side of the road stand the massive greystone mills that provided work and wages for whole families (my own among them) from the warren of hillside terraces.

Not all the streets on these old maps are named. Among those that are I found some that appeared in the census against my ancestors' names. Never owners, always tenants, they lived at two addresses in High Street, then in Middle Road before moving close to the top of the hill in the grand sounding but equally overcrowded Hanover Square.

I went to walk in their footsteps and stand outside the doors where they once stood – as I had done so tremulously some months earlier when discovering my tree's paternal branch in southern Wales.

It was not to be. The roads that bordered this one-time enclave of terrace upon terrace of back-to-back millworker houses are still there. Traces of 19th century buildings remain on the roads that define the area of my search: Cemetery Hill, Boothroyd Lane, Moorlands Road and Huddersfield Road. But within their borders nothing of the past remains. The houses of my forefathers have been bulldozed and replaced by what the English term a council estate – subsidised housing for the economically disadvantaged, the unemployed and the dispossessed.

High Street and Middle Road, where the maternal side of my family once lived, remain in name only. Along their footpaths walk swarthy bearded men in flowing white robes, women secreted behind burqas, veils and yashmaks, young boys in baggy pantaloons clutching prayer books on their way to the mosques. The corner stores and takeaways are run by Asian families selling Asian fare. Our car's slow trawl as I searched for the tiniest remnant of my personal history aroused hostile stares. I was the suspicious and unwelcome stranger even though generations of my family had worked long and arduously to eke out a living on this same steep Yorkshire hillside.

At least I had the consolation next day, in the garden surrounding Dewsbury Minster, of finding several tombstones – now preserved as flagstones forming the garden's paths – in memory of various Newsomes. Dewsbury may have obliterated our former homes to house its newcomers but at least it has ensured our name lives on.

THOSE DARK SATANIC MILLS

HANNAH Newsome dipped deep into the basin and gathered a dollop of dripping on to the knife. She made sure the creamy fat covered every bit of the two thick slices of bread laid out on the kitchen table. That done, she sprinkled plenty of salt over the greasy spread then covered each slice with another slab of bread. She sometimes wondered whether it was the actual dripping her husband liked or the salty coating he demanded she give it.

Either way, at least he would have something substantial inside him to sustain him through the long and arduous hours on the mill floor, not like many of her neighbours' men where money for food was often hard to find. A man needed something solid inside him to keep out the cold and give him the energy to survive another shift. Hard work never hurt anyone but a man had to have food and sleep to survive it.

Hannah wiped her hands down her apron, wrapped the sandwiches in a sheet of brown paper and pushed the package across to her husband. There was another for young Jonathan and another for Mary, still unmarried at 23 and spending back–breaking hours as a wool machine feeder.

'There you are, love. That'll keep you going.'

They were familiar words; a daily recitative. John Newsome gulped the last mouthful of tannin-black tea from his enamel mug and pushed the sandwiches into the baggy pocket of his roughly woven woollen jacket. Son and daughter echoed his actions.

'Reckon we'd best be off then or they'll be docking our wages.' More ritual words.

'And we rightly can't afford that,' said Hannah. 'There's hardly enough for food and rent as it is. The sooner you get that overlooker job the better it'll be for all o' us.'

She was saying nothing new. John had heard it all before; many times. He knew the truth of her statement and would change it if he could. The reality was that Hannah's hopes were unlikely to be realised. Maybe the next generation would fare better. Already young Jonathan was learning a trade as a dyer and might well improve his prospects if he applied himself and got to know all the tricks of the business.

John shrugged, shaking his coat further up his shoulders, gathering it around him against the icy December blasts coming down off Dewsbury Moor. The wind whined through the gaps around the door that led directly on to the narrow alley separating their terraced cottage from an identical row across the cobbled alley.

'Aye, love, a bit more brass would help.'

It was a tired acknowledgement of a well-worn plaint. There was nothing he could do to change things. One simply lived in hope. If others had moved up from the mill floor to being one of the overseers, so could he. But the muck heap of employment had a massive base and only a few hardy souls conquered the steep slope to its narrow pinnacle. He would do his job, put in a fair day's work for what was regarded as a fair day's pay, make no trouble (unlike those union rabble-rousers) and trust that his efforts would eventually be recognised.

He moved out of the lamp's low light and into the shadows by the door.

'Right, I'll be off then.'

'And you take care; there's too many getting killed and injured by those machines.'

The Industrial Revolution that had transformed the north of England from a maze of cottage industries into grimy cities clogged with factories was still a dangerous stranger to the thousands who had been forced to work on the mills' massive machines. Centuries of home-based trades had been obliterated within the span of a single generation. Workplace safety was an unknown concept; there were no protective grilles.

'Look at that poor man last week who got caught in the machine at Senior's Mill,' cautioned Hannah. 'They thought he was dead. Fact is, he's lucky to be alive.'

'Aye, love, I'll take care,' said John, his tone dismissive of her concern, even though he was all too well aware of the high mortality rate among the mill workers. Accidents always happened to someone else.

The door squeaked as John tugged it ajar from where it had swollen against the frame with all the recent rain that had left the Calder River overflowing and flooding many of the mills lining its banks. Jonathan and Mary were close behind him as he stepped into the early morning damp and dark at 5.30am. There was mud and debris everywhere and even the bodies of drowned sheep washed down from the moors in the deluge.

There were muffled greetings as they fell into step with neighbours all trudging the same muddy route to the mills and dye works spread out along the riverbank at the bottom of the hill.

For John it led him along to Cemetery Road and down the steep slope to Huddersfield Road. From there it was another mile to heavily industrial Ravensthorpe, a boom region of the mid-1800s where mills and houses were hurriedly built to cash in on the region's newfound status as a centre of the international woollen trade.

John Newsome was just one of a throng of sleep-deprived automatons – men, women and children – going through the drudgery of a daily routine from which few would ever escape. Their hours were long and their jobs tedious and repetitive.

Hannah fared no better. She was not far behind John as she left to go to her work as a wool keeler, still hoping against hope that the family would one day lift themselves a rung or two up the economic ladder and away from the depressing over-crowding of their back-to-back terrace in Middle Road. How pleased she had been when they had moved from nearby High Street a couple of years ago. At least they no longer had to contend with the screams and brawls from the brothel two doors away and the pub on the nearby corner.

Hannah was three hours into her shift when the foreman called her away from her work, his face a mixture of displeasure and concern. The news was bad so he supposed he should let her go, even though the managers had told him to make sure everyone put in a full day's work.

'There's been an accident,' he said with true Yorkshire bluntness. 'Your man. He's been hurt. Badly, they say.'

Hannah's shocked face discomfited him. He shuffled about on his feet. He reached out to help her wind her coat and scarf about her.

'Here,' he said. 'Take the tram.'

She felt the coin her palm, surprised by the man's concern, still dazed by the urgency of his message. She scampered out past the lines of looms, unaware of the faces turned towards her. News spread quickly, especially bad news.

A huddle of men was awaiting her at the Ravensthorpe mill. They hurried her inside. John Newsome was huddled up on the floor laid out on a pile of rags, his own clothing torn and ripped all the way down one side, his bloodied ribs showing through.

Hannah's hands went to her face, covering her mouth to smother an involuntary scream.

'Oh my God,' was all that came out. Twice. A double horror-stricken gasp. She bent closer over her husband's immobile body, trying to make sense of what she was seeing.

She looked up at the cluster of men circling her.

'Can't you do something? Where's the doctor?'

A tall, frock-coated man stepped forward, a walking stick in one hand.

'I am Doctor Marsden,' he announced. His manner was haughty; his voice pompous.

He prodded John Newsome's prone form with his stick. His voice was gruff, lacking any warmth. John groaned, trying to protest at the indignity of the doctor's proddings but too maimed to speak.

'Take him home,' the doctor said. 'Keep applying hot wet cloths on him.'

'Is that all?' asked Hannah. 'Can't you do something? Look at him, he's bleeding. He's in terrible pain.'

The doctor, a man in his fifties, looked at her dispassionately, almost disdainfully.

'I'll call on you tomorrow morning.'

The doctor's tone was dismissive, impatient. He may be a member of the Royal College of Surgeons and the Licensed Society of Apothecaries, but none of that expertise was going to be expended on the limp and supine figure at his feet. This was just another inevitable accident with an inevitable outcome. It happened all the time. It was not his problem. He turned away and said a few low words to the mill manager then waved his stick in the direction of his groom, standing dutifully in the doorway.

'Stand by Cayworth; we'll be leaving soon.'

A few moments later, he was as good as his word. Hannah, still kneeling over John's body, looked up at the foreman.

'What happened?'

'As best we can tell, his smock got caught in't machine.' He indicated a thin young man Hannah had noticed hovering behind the man's shoulder.

'Young Joseph here did what he could. The lad stopped machine reet awa' but 'twas too late.'

The youth nodded in agreement, his face drained of all colour, his hands twitching at the corners of his own smock.

'It was terrible missus, terrible. I could do nowt.'

Throughout the night, John Newsome lapsed in and out of consciousness, feverish and shivering, groaning with the pain as Hannah dutifully followed the doctor's orders and swaddled her husband in cloths soaked in hot water, although she could see little sense or benefit in what she was doing. At some time in the middle of the night Mary persuaded her mother to sleep for a couple of hours while she continued the swabbing and bathing of her father's wounds.

Hannah roused herself when the timekeeper passed on his rounds, tapping on windows and doors to make sure workers were awake and on time for the start of another day's hard labour down in the mills and dyeworks.

'There'll be no work for me today,' she said to Mary. 'But you and Jonathan had best be off or there'll be no money coming in. Anyhow, I've to wait for that doctor. Maybe he'll do summat today instead of poking yer poor pa with his stick.'

Hannah waited many more hours, through the lightening gloom of the winter's morning and on through the sunless day beneath lowering clouds and it was only as what little light there was began to fade in mid–afternoon that Doctor Marsden made his promised appearance. He said little other than to maintain the treatment.

'But he's not eating, doctor,' said Hannah. 'He's had nowt since the accident.'

The doctor sniffed.

'That's to be expected,' he said without explaining why.

Over the following days, Hannah watched her wounded husband weaken and fade. She slowly accepted the reality of the situation. She nursed him while knowing it would do little good. A fever racked his whole body; one moment he would break out in immense sweats and minutes later he would be shaking with the shivers of intense cold. He moaned in agony as he tried to move stiffening muscles. Spasms that gripped his jaw and neck worsened daily and spread to his upper body. Hannah held mugs of soup to his lips but he couldn't swallow. The metal that had ripped his body was now acting as a poison.

Doctor Marsden visited briefly again two days later, on the Saturday, and again the following Monday and Wednesday. By then Hannah had done her own diagnosis and hardly needed Marsden's confirmation that her husband had been smitten by the deadly lockjaw, the tetanus of modern times. She called on a friend, John Connon from nearby Back High Street, a sturdy stonemason, who confirmed her worst fears.

By Friday she knew the end was close; she could feel John's life ebbing from him as she clasped his hand. Doctor Marsden visited twice that day, almost showing concern and compassion but acknowledging with a shake of his head there was nothing he could do.

'His injuries were too bad right from the start,' he said. 'The cuts were too deep.'

My great-great-grandfather, John Newsome, died at 6.30 that Friday evening, December 23, 1868, a sad Christmas for his family, and was taken by neighbours to the nearby Prince Albert Inn to await an inquest. Here there was space and cooling for the body to be laid out uncovered and in full view of a jury that formed its amateur opinion of the cause of death. There were no professional pathologists in those days to give more informed assessments.

Next morning, Christmas Eve, Coroner for Yorkshire Thomas Taylor travelled over from his home on Margaret Street in Wakefield and held a brief and businesslike inquest. He saw that Hannah was seated at the table's end and addressed her gently.

'This is a sad and difficult time for you but the law requires me to ask questions and take a statement from you.'

She nodded in understanding and gathered her shawl tightly around her. Jonathan and Martha stood behind her, each with a comforting hand on her shoulder, their faces grim and knowing what lay ahead. Their house was tied to the mill where John Newsome worked and died; they would have to move yet again and find somewhere else to rent.

Hannah answered the Coroner's questions in a low voice that hardly wavered. She made a point of mentioning Doctor Marsland's attitude and the gaps between his attendances. Mr Taylor wrote it down in his notebook. It took less than a page.

Joseph Stocks was the only other witness. The 17–year–old dyer's apprentice gave his address as Dewsbury Moor and said he had worked with John Newsome for the past 18 months. Coroner Taylor led him into his evidence.

'And what happened on Wednesday the ninth of December?'

'I began work with him and others about half past six of the clock,' said young Stocks. 'We had oil lamps.'

'And ….?' The Coroner let his question hang in the crowded room.

'About an hour afterward a window was blown down and fell on a machine on which the cotton is dyed.'

He turned his eyes briefly towards the body of John Newsome laid out on the nearby table.

'I asked him to help me to lift up the sash.'

Again his gaze flickered to his dead mentor as if seeking guidance in retelling events.

'He stretched over the machine and we lifted the sash up. Mr Newsome slipped forward and fell on the machine which caught his smock in the cog wheels.'

His words now tumbled out in a rush as if to match the pace of his action.

'I ran and got the engine stopped. The machine was not running.'

There was a heavy silence in the room. Hannah's head was bowed, hiding the tears on her cheeks. Joseph Stocks swallowed, gagging on his words, recalling the horror of the moment.

'When you are ready …' the Coroner urged.

'Yes, well, he was caught by the shafting. He was twisted around the upright shaft. His clothes had to be cut off.'

His words came to an abrupt stop. They hung in the air, each person in the room imagining the scene he had described.

'Thank you, Mr Stocks; that will be all. If you'd please sign here …'

The young man scrawled his name on the Coroner's notebook and moved back into the crowd. Two women covered John Newsome's body with a sheet. The Coroner added briefly to his notes and addressed the room.

'I find that the deceased, John Newsome, died as a result of wounds received in an accident at the mill. The verdict is accidentally injured.'

He closed his book, stood up, directed a sympathetic nod at Hannah and left the room. The Newsomes, including my 16-year-old great-grandfather Jonathan, were left to spend Christmas burying their man and start facing a future with one less wage and the search for somewhere else to live.

DIVERSIONS AND DETOURS

THE route into the past is long and winding, full of distractions and dead-ends. Family historians are faced with a continual dilemma – to stay on the main road or allow themselves to be lured down tempting byways.

There is no set rule; the choice is personal and individual. It is a matter of deciding how close you want to remain to the trunk of the family tree and how much time and effort you want to expend venturing out along the branches and even the twigs, shooting off in all directions.

Sometimes, however, there is no choice: the decision is forced upon you by the tangle of timber blocking your path.

Such was the case with the Hooleys. They arrived by marriage and stayed to blight my tree with their presence over several decades – a rogue graft that no amount of pruning could shift.

They became an infestation, clinging on in different guises. Frustratingly I could find no one else interested in researching the Hooley line. The name provoked no interest on help lines and forums despite them being a prolific breed in Derbyshire, Lancashire and Cheshire in the early 19th century.

This was one of those instances where a family historian has little choice but to succumb to the diversion. My research showed the Hooleys had twice married into my maternal line and produced various ancestors. They were also lodgers and neighbours of my forebears. This was therefore one of those detours that had to be taken.

Eventually, persistence and an Ancestry message board response unmasked the most mysterious of the Hooleys and provided another fascinating glimpse into my family's past and gave me a great grand uncle of dubious repute.

James and Elizabeth Hooley either had high hopes or a great sense of irony when they named their second child Major Ernest. As the son of a Lancashire engine-smith in the mid-1800s, he had few prospects of ever achieving any sort or rank, military or otherwise. By investing him at birth they endowed him with a status he never earned but often misused

'Hi, I'm Major Hooley,' was an introduction that, while strictly true, could easily deceive the many gullible young women who had the misfortune to attract his attention into thinking he was a man of substance. His history is littered with widows and abandoned wives, unexplained children and a confusion of relationships. He intruded into my life by marrying great-aunt Fanny Newsome and thus by default became another leaf on the family tree – and a blighted one at that. Such is his history that it comes as little surprise that no one has emerged to admit to an interest in exploring the Hooley line. An impoverished, illiterate womaniser is not the preferred choice of ancestor.

When, in 1868, 10-year-old Fanny was coping with the shocking workplace death of her father, Major Hooley was already married to Martha Bennett and living a few doors away from the Newsomes in Middle Road, Dewsbury. The Hooleys' son, Joseph, lived just three years and Martha died six years later, almost 10 years to the day that Fanny watched her father's painful death.

With characters such as this to be discovered it sometimes pays to be lured away from the highways of history and take the winding and less travelled country lanes.

HOOLEY DOOLEY, HERE COMES THE MAJOR

THE funeral was short and simple; almost brutal in its brevity. It was a necessity, a far too frequent occurrence for the folk crammed into the hillside terraces overlooking the murky Calder River. It was not something to lavish any hard-earned money on.

Major Hooley had buried his three-year-old son Joseph in 1872. Now, six years later, on a bitter November day, he was laying wife Martha to rest. He had watched her rapidly decline over the past four months, her body becoming more and more bloated, her face puffy and pallid – the ghostly white of death. He understood little of the medical jargon the doctors spouted at him but he recognised the air of futility and finality in their treatment. Everyone knew their living conditions were formidable weapons against relief or recovery from her illness.

The burial was a bleak occasion. It was made all the more drear by the perfunctory attitude of the vicar and the pallbearers. Everyone had become hardened to death; it rarely shocked or surprised. No family was immune from the diseases and disasters that formed the fabric of their existence.

Major Hooley accepted the condolences of family and friends as he walked away from the grave. Following close behind was his sister, Elizabeth, with baby daughter Alice cradled in her arms and three-year-old Joseph clinging to the folds of her coat. Around Elizabeth's shoulder was the protective arm of her husband, my great-grandfather Jonathan Newsome.

Also nearby were Jonathan's mother Hannah and his sister Fanny, neighbours of the Hooleys on many occasions as the two families moved from one rented hovel to another. They had become much closer entwined with the marriage of Jonathan and Elizabeth in 1872.

'A sad day, Mr Hooley,' said Hannah.

'Aye, indeed, and no doubt there'll be many more before winter's done.'

'She suffered bravely, poor soul.'

'She did that,' Major agreed. 'But there was nowt could be done once the poison took hold. It was terrible to see her like that.'

'You did your best.'

'And so did you and young Fanny there.' He doffed his cap towards the young woman at Hannah's side. 'She was a great strength.'

Fanny acknowledged his words with a coy smile. Even after spending so many painful hours in close company with him as she helped him nurse his ailing wife, she still found him daunting and disturbing. Maybe it was his feeling of helplessness as he watched her changing Martha's dressings and swabbing her swollen limbs that had made him somewhat brusque and forbidding.

'It's woman's business,' Major would say, leaving her alone with his wife sweating and groaning as the dropsy spread through her body from her rapidly failing kidneys. He seemed unable to look at Martha's swollen face and her bulbous ankles with their weeping sores. Fanny sensed his impatience with Martha's cries of pain as she clutched at her abdomen. She put it down to anger at the living conditions that made such diseases so prevalent, and tried to ignore his peevish behavior. Yet she had seen a tender side to him amid all the frustration and fury; like the times he had mopped Martha's brow or held her up to sip the herbal concoctions some of the older women recommended.

Major was eight years older than her, a married man, a father and now a widower – not someone she found easy company, no matter how much she wanted to comfort him and ease his distress. He had buried one child and now had to care for two motherless girls, five-year-old Sarah Ann and two-year-old Martha, named after the woman they had just buried. How could anyone not feel sorrow for one who had suffered so much?

She stole another glance at him as they quickened their pace away from the burial mound. She dared to give him a comforting smile.

'The doctor said it's the damp,' she commented.

'Aye there'll be no end to it if we canna get warm or dry our clothes and bedding,' said Major. 'There's nowt can be done in this weather and with these houses.'

He waved his arm in a wide arc that embraced all their surroundings – the cramped rows of back-to-back terraces, the smoke stacks of the factories threading their way through the valley below, the lowering clouds and the gentle drizzle that even now was seeping into clothes that would never be properly dried or aired throughout the damp dark months of winter.

'Aye, indeed,' said Hannah. 'It's what we've been born into. You have to accept it.'

'And why should we? So many dying before their time.'

'Maybe, but we don't forget them. It's ten years since I buried John and I remember it like it was yesterday.'

Major sniffed. He found such thoughts morbid; they were not for him. Life was bad enough without dwelling on the past and the dead. He had the future to cope with. However, now was not the time for expressing a contrary view.

'Aye, it takes a while,' he said. 'Your John was a good man.'

Hannah kept step, her arm linked in that of Fanny's, as they moved to the churchyard gate and Cemetery Road.

'And what will you do now, Mr Hooley?'

He looked perplexed by her question. What more was there to do? He would attend the inevitable wake where morbid talk among the guests would turn maudlin or merry depending on how they handled their drink.

And tomorrow he would join the pre-dawn trail of workers snaking down into the town as he returned to his job as a blanket raiser. For hours on end he would stand at his machine as lengths of cloth turned on their rollers while he made sure the teasels, the wire brushes, raised a pile on the fabric and ensured an even nap on the surface.

Hannah recognised his puzzlement.

'I mean about your home life; the girls? That's not a job for a man.'

'You're right there, missus. Truth to say I haven't given it much thought what with everything else that's been going on. The poor mites'll have to fend for themselves 'til I get home of a night, I suppose.'

He shrugged; that was how things were.

'There's plenty of others in the same boat,' he said.

'And you don't want to join them,' said Hannah firmly. 'Girls aren't like boys. You can't turn them loose; they'll need someone to look after them.'

She kept her eyes focused firmly on the path ahead but Fanny felt the firm squeeze of her mother's arm on hers. The prompt was clear.

'Perhaps I could help,' she said meekly. 'The girls are used to me. I can dress them and make sure they get summat to eat.'

Major gave her one of those penetrating looks she found so disturbing and difficult to interpret; assessing and appraising without giving any clue as to his thoughts or conclusions. It was the sort of look she'd seen farmers give to cattle and sheep when they came down off the moors and gathered in town on market days: evaluating and judging their worth.

'Aye,' he said. 'That'll be reet good. The girls are missing their ma.'

He fixed his look on Fanny.

'A man could do a lot worse.'

She blushed and clung tighter to her mother's arm. Hannah took control.

'We'll see what we can arrange,' she said. 'Fanny's not working full time; the mill's got little need for doublers at the present.'

They had reached the big iron double gates of the cemetery. Clusters of other mourners were following behind. Hannah and Fanny paused and turned left to head down the hill to Ingham Road. Major extended his hand to Hannah and then to Fanny.

'Thank you for coming today and for your help with Martha.'

Fanny acknowledged his gesture with a nod and a demure smile. There was something about him; maybe it would be good to help with his daughters; certainly a change from standing at the doubling machine, twisting the strands of wool together to make a single yarn.

'Perhaps we will see you soon, Mr Hooley,' said Hannah, giving Fanny's arm another secret squeeze as they walked away towards the damp and dreary hovel they called home.

Many of the same people who had been in the churchyard on that bleak November day, gathered a mere eight months later on July 14, 1879, at St Matthew's Church in Dewsbury's West Town for the wedding of Fanny Newsome to Major Hooley. It was the finale to what is usually described as a whirlwind romance. However, such romance as had taken place had been hurried and perfunctory as Fanny slipped into her role of surrogate mother to Sarah Ann and Martha. Marriage seemed inevitable more for appearances than for love as she spent more and more time under the Hooley roof.

Behind the determined smiles of the main players lay the realities of the occasion. Major, a working man struggling to cope with the needs of two young children, had found in Fanny a carer, cook and comforter for himself and his daughters. Hannah, a widow battling to survive, had divested herself of her adult daughter and had one less mouth to feed. And the daughter, Fanny, had lost the stigma of the spinster label by gaining the perceived security of a husband and a home.

And so it was that St Matthew's – built in 1849 as part of the 600 Churches campaign and nowadays doing duty as luxury apartments – played host to a reasonably happy occasion. Certainly there's every reason to assume the newlyweds celebrated long and lustily for Fanny was soon heavy with child, giving birth to son Edward nine months after walking down the aisle.

And there the romance, or any pretence of it, came to an abrupt end. Fanny's decision to go home to mum in High Street for Edward's birth was not unusual. There she stayed while Major not only remained at Ranter's Hill with his daughters but also had the effrontery to describe himself in the 1881 census less than a year later as a widower, although his wife was very much alive and still living with mum. To him, Fanny had ceased to exist.

Indeed she seemed to disappear completely. There was no mention of her in the 1891 census, although mum Hannah was alive and kicking, "living on her own means" at 105 Huddersfield Road, two doors down from the West Town Inn that was once one of the town's liveliest and most popular drinking holes.

Major, however, was a survivor, moving on from address to address – one of them in Huddersfield Road close to Hannah's abode – and briefly becoming a grandfather to Sarah's daughter Cooper who died on January 12, 1883, at the age of two from chest and throat infections. Not surprisingly for a man who could probably sweet talk his way out of any situation, Major quit work in the mills and tried to make a living as a hawker, spruiking his wares around the streets of Dewsbury until his death in 1905 at the early age of 57.

His Hooley line lives on. But that is a story for others to tell.

CHANGING FROM LOOM TO SHOVEL

JONATHAN Newsome stuck his thumbs in behind the thick leather belt buckled around his waist, fingers clenched tight over his waistband. He was far from pleased with what he had to say. Wife Elizabeth couldn't hide her distress, unable to stop wringing her hands together. Son Joseph looked disconsolate. He knew full well what was coming but resolved to stay strong.

'There's nowt for it, son,' said Jonathan. 'It's the only way. There's jobs going over at Chidswell colliery and they'll take you on. Start Monday.'

Joseph knew the truth of his father's blunt words but that didn't make them any more acceptable. He could see his mother shared his anguish.

'It's not what I want, either,' said his father. 'Believe me, I've done my best but the work's not there in the mill.'

He reached out and laid a consoling hand on Joseph's shoulder. The lad shuddered, close to tears.

'I'd be reet pleased to have you working alongside me,' said Jonathan, 'but… '

He shrugged; his voice trailed off. They were going over familiar ground, looking for hope where none existed. It was inevitable that Joseph would start his working life as a miner, deep underground at one of the town's 32 collieries. A decline in the wool trade meant he would be unable to follow in the family footsteps working in the mills that had sustained the Newsomes for three generations. His father tried to console him.

'It's for the best,' he said. 'And think on it, lad, there's more brass to be made down the pit than in the mill.'

'Aye, that's as maybe,' chimed in Elizabeth, 'but think of the danger.'

'And you reckon there's nowt dangerous about working in the mills,' retorted Jonathan. 'There's some poor bugger being killed or injured there almost every day. It didn't do my dad much good.'

Elizabeth shuddered and kept twisting her hands in her lap, her brow creased with concern, her anxiety palpable. Jonathan may be trying to erase some of her fears but his comment unleashed other emotions; it was a blunt reminder of the several days he had spent watching his father die from wounds received when he was dragged into machinery at the dye works.

'But the pit's so far underground,' she said. 'You can be days trapped as well as injured.'

She threw a worried glance at her husband. Both were still trying to come to terms with Joseph's impending shift from schoolboy to miner, a brutal transition into manhood at the tender age of 14. The lad shrugged and tried to put some gloss on the gloom.

'I'll learn a trade,' he said. 'Work my way up. Make summat of myself.'

His parents smiled briefly. His acceptance of the situation was more than they had hoped for. On the other hand, it was what was expected in homes where every able–bodied person was obliged to work and contribute to the family coffers. Every penny counted. Although two years younger than her brother, Alice Newsome was already toiling every day as a weaver. As was the young boarder, Sarah Castle, they had taken in to supplement their meagre income. And neither marriage nor childbirth would put an end to their ceaseless routines.

The best that Jonathan and Elizabeth could hope for was that Joseph would achieve his goal and eventually rise sufficiently up the ladder to be employed above ground and not have to face that daily descent into a dust–laden and gaseous hell. They knew, however, that opportunities to rise above the ruck were few and far between among the mass of lowly-paid workers who kept the mills and mines turning out their precious commodities. They and their parents and all their widespread family had spent their lives in menial tasks.

Joseph's parents knew coal mining was risky at best and suicidal at worst. There was danger at every turn and it was said of some jobs that a man needed to have a death wish to do them. A colliery fireman, for example, was expected to crawl through the tunnel holding a lighted candle attached to a long stick in order to explode any dangerous, flammable gases that might have accumulated ahead of him. Only in fairly recent times had the advent of trade unions meant an easing of some of the extreme working conditions – so extreme that workers who resisted could not only find themselves locked out of their workplace but also be barred from the employer-owned hovels where they lived.

'Let's be thankful it's now and not fifty years ago,' said Jonathan. 'Things were right bad back then.'

Early 19th century legislation aimed at curtailing child labour had proved to be unenforceable and it was not until 1833 that the first effective law was passed appointing factory inspectors to ensure the law was being obeyed. Conditions in coalmines were often terrible with children as young as five working underground Some sort of enlightenment occurred in 1842 with the passing of a law lifting the minimum age to ten and banning all females from working underground.

It also prevented children under nine from working in textile factories and decreed that children aged nine to thirteen must not work for more than twelve hours a day or forty-eight hours a week. In addition, they had to receive at least two hours' education a day, although it wasn't until 1880 that schooling became mandatory.

Teenagers were not so fortunate under the 1842 legislation: kids aged from thirteen to eighteen could still work up to sixty-nine hours a week. Their one consolation was that there was to be no more night work as nobody under 18 was allowed to work between 8.30pm and 5.30am.

Gradually things got better: in 1844 a law banned all children under eight from working and the 1847 Factory Act said that women and children could only work ten hours a day in textile factories.

Up until 1850, weaving was a home industry with children helping to supplement the family business. When the factory system put an end to home weaving these children were pushed out into the spinning mills as soon as employers would take them. Five- and six-year-old children could be forced to work ten or twelve hours a day. Supervisors would beat them if they were late or showed signs of slacking. Some were even strapped to their machines. Accidents were frequent and deformities a common infliction.

In 1867, the law was extended to all factories, a factory being defined as a place where more than 50 people were employed in manufacturing and thus leaving the door open to the many cottage industries and sweatshops surrounding the wool trade to continue their onerous workplace practices.

Gradually the workers such as Jonathan Newsome's father (my great-great-grandfather) began flexing their muscles and making their own demands rather than waiting for the slow moving legislators to do something about their appalling working conditions. However, although skilled craftsmen combined in the 1850s and 1860s to form national trade unions, their unskilled colleagues such as the Newsome brood did not become organised until the late 1880s.

It was a long trudge for young Joseph from the family home in Middle Road, Dewsbury, to the colliery at Ossett where once rolling farmlands were scarred with a conglomeration of pits and mineshafts, many of them hastily sunk and poorly maintained. He was far from alone; the rush to open mines had lured many men up the Wakefield Road hill from Dewsbury and there was a steady flow of Ossett people going in the other direction on their way to work in the mills.

By happy coincidence, the hotel I stayed at during my journey into the Newsomes' past bordered a large tract of open land flowing down into a valley and up the hillside to Owl Lane where Joseph began his mining career. Here, on the Dewsbury-Ossett border, some thirty collieries employed hundreds of men and boys to scour the earth below. All traces of the mines they worked in have been long removed; the shafts safely filled and secured. Sports fields and walking tracks, shops and houses fill this once grimy industrial wasteland.

Nothing remains to tell of the arduous toil, immense danger and pitiful conditions the miners endured. Unlike the joy of my explorations into the Welsh side of the family, there was to be no retracing of an ancestor's footsteps here.

However, the drive by car from where the Newsomes' home once stood, through Dewsbury and up the long winding incline to my base at the solid old Heath Cottage Hotel, left little doubt about the durability and endurance of young Joseph. It is almost beyond belief that this teenager made such a trek, twice a day and often in miserable weather, and on top of a brutally physical day's labour of ten hours or more. Yet this was part and parcel of my ancestors' lives a mere two generations ago.

Elizabeth held back her tears as she sent her son off to begin his life as a miner. Jonathan stayed as stoic as ever, briefly gripping Joseph's arm and giving him a solid pat on the back.

'Take care, son, and find yer sen a mate,' he said. 'They'll look after yer.'

Joseph arrived at the pit gates with some idea of what to expect. He had talked to other miners and listened to their stories and advice. Accidents and deaths were recalled and accepted as inevitable; the best one could do was to remain alert and pray that it wasn't your turn to be maimed or killed. The one consolation was that the take-home pay of those who survived to work another day was well above that of the average worker in other trades.

First day nerves quickly heightened into something close to sheer terror as Joseph was herded with a group of men into an iron cage. Not all the blasé talk in the world from old hands could prepare him for this. The gates clanged shut. An overhead pulley whirred as stout ropes unwound and they began their descent 150 metres down the brick-lined shaft into a darkness only dimly lit by the miners' flickering lamps. Joseph held tightly on to the metal rail as the cage juddered and shook, guided only by "thimbles" working on wire conductors 40mm in diameter. Slowly he relaxed as he took comfort from the calm manner of those clustered close to him. From now on, this was how every day would begin and end – if he survived down below.

Joseph was one of more than 200 men and boys working underground at the Chidswell Colliery. Another 40 or so – managers, engineers and supervisors – enjoyed the relative luxury of surface work. A handful of larger mines were spread over the Ossett landscape – one with more than six hundred men hewing away underground – but most were fairly small operations that often had fairly brief lifespans, some of them employing fewer than a dozen miners. Shafts could descend to as little as 100 metres below the surface before finding coal bearing seams; others were sunk to 350 metres or more. The shafts were a mere four metres in diameter and the tunnels leading off them were even narrower with no room for a man to stand upright.

The talk among the men that morning was the usual mix: the football, the dismal weather, strife at home and whinges about the bosses. Wages and conditions were a constant theme, spurred on by a growth in trade unionism and the gradual realisation that uncompromising conditions could be resisted and changed.

There had already been a strike over at Gawthorpe Colliery where thirty miners downed tools in demand for a ten per cent wage rise. Other colliery owners had agreed to pay the increase but Gawthorpe's owners, the Haigh family, had refused. Levies were imposed on miners at other collieries and subscriptions were collected to support the men on strike.

'That's only the start of it,' predicted one voice out of the gloom. 'Price of coal's falling so bosses will start cutting wages.'

'They can cut their own wages before they cut ours,' said another, a statement greeted with grunts of approval.

'Yeah, we're the ones doing the work,' chimed in a third. 'Let 'em come down here and do a shift or two and see if we earn our money.'

Miners were, however, already earning forty per cent above the standard worker's rate thanks to the efforts of the increasingly militant Miners Federation of Great Britain. The owners, represented by the Coalowners Federation, saw this as scope for cutting wages while still keeping miners' pay above the community norm.

'It's the fifties all over again,' warned the first speaker. 'You mark my words.'

His remark meant nothing to Joseph but as he crawled through the tunnels shovelling or using his hands to pitch the freshly hewn coal into wagons and troughs he listened and learned from the older men.

They had been there in the early weeks of 1858 when news spread that Waterloo Colliery's owner, Kirby Fenton, had told his workers he was cutting their wages because of poor times ahead. Other mines followed, even though most were already working only four days a week. The miners refused to work at lower wages and went on strike. Men at nearby pits agreed to pay a levy to support them.

A meeting of employers on February 23 decided on a fifteen per cent wage cut for all employees of the West Yorkshire Coalowners Association. On March 29 the miners accepted the wage cut, but decided to form a union and stage strikes at three selected mines, with a levy of two shillings a week to support the men on strike.

After an unsuccessful attempt to bring in surface workers and farmers as black labour to reopen their pits the colliery owners gave a month's notice that they would close all mines in the area to cut off the source of relief funds. On October 7, 1858, more than three thousand men were locked out of the mines and their colliery owned homes.

Despite the miners and their families suffering immense hardships, it was the owners who broke first. Public sympathy was with the miners; it was cold and there was a shortage of coal, so prices were high. Such conditions led to compromise.

On November 26, 1858, Mr Garside of the Leeds Colliery offered to allow the men to start working with a seven per cent wage cut. He promised to rescind some of the most hated bylaws and not insist that the miners abandon the union. The miners accepted the offer and by the end of the week all other employers had offered similar terms and the strike ended after 36 weeks.

'I can see it all happening again,' said one of the men hacking at the seam alongside Joseph. 'We saw it in 1869, too; almost no work then. The pattern's the same. You wait and see.'

On a July day three years later, in 1893, after one of the driest three months recorded in the British Isles, Joseph joined the throng outside the colliery gates waiting to hear from the Miners Federation representatives. The thunderous clouds lowering overhead were ominous; a portent of sudden and drastic change. The union called on its members to down tools. It said the employers' revised demand to pay only fifteen per cent above the standard rate – an effective reduction in wages of twenty-five per cent – was not acceptable. The heavens opened and launched a deluge of hail and rain that was to last for nine hours.

Joseph turned to the man at his side.

'Surely summat's better than nothing,' he said.

'And nothing's what we'll end up with if we don't fight,' came the staunch reply.

Joseph wasn't convinced. He shivered and pulled his jacket over his head. He was already drenched; even being down the pit was better than standing out on this bleak hillside. The family needed his wages. He needed his wages.

In the early stages of the dispute, the coffers of the Yorkshire Miners Association were able to pay nine shillings a week to each man laid off. This was soon cut back to seven shillings a week but the association's meagre resources rapidly dwindled and the last strike pay was handed over way back on September 22 – a bleak Friday for everyone.

As the strike dragged on, Joseph had started walking out with Sarah Kelly, a young lass one year his junior whom he had come to know when her family lived a few doors away from the Newsomes at their previous home in Back Hanover Street. The Kellys still lived close by, in John Street, and the pair began meeting and idling away the time in the long summer evenings when no one wanted to be confined inside their overcrowded and airless cottages.

When the dispute extended into autumn and the days grew shorter and colder, Joseph and Sarah looked more to the weekends rather than the evenings for their brief times together. And always he felt frustrated and angry at the endless struggle to save a few precious pennies so that he could buy her a soda or an ice cream. Sarah would try to console him.

'Dinna worry, luv,' she said. 'Ma lets me keep a little for meself. And the strike canna go on forever.'

But Joseph wanted money of his own. The longer the strike continued, the harder things became. The family needed his wages and he wanted to feel the jingle of coins in his pocket. Work at any price seemed preferable to all these idle hours, days and weeks in the hope of a minor improvement in their conditions.

And he didn't like the constant talk of fighting. He took little encouragement from his father's many lectures to the family on how the workers needed to stick together and shuddered at the retelling of some ugly moments at the mills when police had been called. He huddled in alongside others seeking shelter under a massive oak tree. With all this gloom about it was little wonder that there had also been such a sudden and dramatic end to the long spell of warm dry weather. Cold, wind and rain suited the prevailing mood.

The strike hit the local economy hard because of its reliance on coal as a fuel for industry and transport. The Great Northern Railway cancelled the majority of its passenger trains between Ossett, Leeds, Wakefield and Bradford. The lack of coal forced textile mills to introduce part-time working and eventually to shut down completely. The Ossett Gas Company increased the price of gas from 2s 9d to 3s 0d a 1000 cubic feet because of the rise in coal prices.

Everywhere he went Joseph sensed aggression and resentment. People were angry that two small Ossett collieries, Healey Lane and Westfield, were working on through the dispute because the men there were not members of the union. Police were called to the Healey Lane pit on Saturday August 12, and again on the following Monday, to prevent a breach of the peace by a group of pickets who stood firm despite the drenching rain sweeping across Yorkshire.

The intimidation worked: by Monday only part of the workforce turned up. Joseph joined the crowd watching the men emerge from the pit. There were hoots and jeers and cries of 'Baa' as the men set off home escorted by police. It was another three weeks before any of the Healey Road miners returned to work, and they again got a hostile reception from a crowd of pickets.

Mill owners tried to keep their businesses going by buying coal from the Durham coalfield and some paid up to triple the normal price. Unfortunately, the coal deliveries were delayed because the North-Eastern Railway was unable to cope with the increase in demand. Some mill owners used coke bought from the Ossett Gas Company instead of coal but by the end of August all the coke stocks had been used up.

Another week, another Monday morning. Jonathan had already left for work at the dye works. Elizabeth busied herself with bundles of bedding. She looked across at Joseph slumped over the table, cradling his mug of tea. The strike had been going six weeks with no end in sight. The relentless daily grind of toiling up the hill to Ossett and waiting around for something to happen was taking its toll on him. As it was on many men and their families. The temptation was to linger at home.

'Let me know if you're going up there today and I'll cut you some bread to take with you,' said Elizabeth.

'I canna decide,' he said, speaking more to the table top than to her. 'Where's the point in it all?'

'You'd better not let your father hear you speak like that. He'll tell you the workers have got to stick together.'

'And where's it getting us?' replied Joseph. 'It'd be better to work for the old wage than having nothing at all.'

'That's as maybe for now, but you've got to think of the future,' said Elizabeth. 'You can't let the bosses break all the agreements.'

She took a loaf of bread from a basket and started sawing off thick chunks. Joseph reluctantly took it as a signal to make a move.

'Perhaps summat will happen up at Westfield today,' he said.

Westfield Colliery was one of the few mines still operating. Owner Henry Westwood not only opposed the wage reduction proposals but decided the local community was best served by supplying coal to keep Ossett's textile mills working and their employees in jobs.

The miners disagreed. A breakaway group of forty or fifty headed towards Westfield and sent pickets in to confront Westwood and demand he close the pit. Westwood refused; after all, he was paying the full wage.

When the pickets reported back, tempers flared. The Westfield miners were hassled as they left the pit and police were called.

Joseph was late home that night.

'We're staying out,' he announced to the family gathered in the gloom of the kitchen. 'We had a meeting. A thousand of us; up at the football field near Ossett railway station.'

He shook his head, rubbed his knuckles into his eyes. Elizabeth thought he looked more down and exhausted than when he was working.

'I still don't understand it though,' said Joseph. 'People getting hurt and there's still no work.'

'Have patience, son,' cautioned Jonathan. 'It might get worse before it gets better. But it's got to be. You mustn't give in.'

'Aye, that's what the preacher told us,' said Joseph. 'A Methodist down from Durham. He reckoned it's a lock-out, not a strike. Real fiery stuff, talking about retribution 'cos the bosses are making fortunes out of the blood of the workers.'

Three days later Joseph fell into step with a great mob of miners marching along the road towards Ossett. There was an air of bravado and aggression in their ranks. Some carried sticks and coshes. Voices were raised in shouts and jeers against the mine owners.

The police were waiting for them on the Ossett boundary at Chidswell, long staves pointed at the miners, truncheons at the ready, some with cutlasses sheathed at their belts. When the police charged, the miners offered little resistance apart from a good deal of stone-throwing and brandishing of sticks.

'It all came to nowt,' Joseph commented to Elizabeth as she stitched a rip in his jacket, received when he snagged it on a bramble in his run from the police.

The days dragged by. Hardship worsened and spread to more families. Strike pay of nine shillings a week to each man was cut back to seven shillings. Then the union ran out of funds. Miners answered the call to another meeting at the football ground and 2000 marched there behind a brass band. Again they resolved to resist any cut in wages but accepted a recommendation from the union that miners return to work at collieries offering the old rate and pay a levy of a shilling a day to support those still in dispute.

Only a minority returned to work as most employers still insisted on a wage reduction. Healey Lane and Pildacre Collieries in Ossett were working double shifts at the beginning of October, while nearby Low Laithes and Roundwood remained closed. Low Laithes management, for example, offered a fifteen per cent reduction in wages rather than the twenty-five per cent reduction of the forty per cent advanced since 1887; and so the miners stayed out.

Four weeks later they gathered yet again, this time in the Temperance Hall to hear miners' association president Edward Cowey – a big man with a big voice – urge them to stand firm and resolute.

It took another month and the intervention of the Prime Minister, William Ewart Gladstone, to bring the bitter dispute to an end. A joint conference held at the Foreign Office on November 17, 1893 between the employers and the union, with Foreign Secretary Lord Rosebery as mediator, agreed to pay the old wage rate until at least February 1, 1894, with a Conciliation Board to follow in at least one year.

The miners at Low Laithes and Roundwood returned to work the following week, the town's mills returned to full production and rail services were gradually restored. And Joseph Newsome resumed his daily trudge up the hill to Chidswell Colliery wondering whether the struggles of the past six months had achieved anything at all and just why he had ever agreed to quit the mills for mining.

DEEP DOWN AND DEADLY

FOR young Joseph Newsome the end of the miners' dispute in November 1893 couldn't have come soon enough. He heaved a huge sigh as he removed his cloth cap and heavy jacket and hung them on the hook behind the door of the family home at 30 Middle Road, Dewsbury.

'Thank God that's all done,' he said. 'Now we can get back to work; put some money on the table.'

His father gave him a comforting pat on his broad shoulders.

'Dinna worry yourself, son. It had to be. We have to go w'out sometimes to make things better. The workers have to stand up to the owners and the bosses.'

Joseph accepted his father's simple philosophy with a shrug. At 18, he was the eldest of six children still living at home along with woollen weaver Sarah Castle, a 20-year-old boarder whose rent helped keep the bailiffs at bay. He and sister Alice, two years his junior and working with Sarah as a mill hand, were expected to contribute to the household budget. Their wages were essential to the weekly purse for food, rent and fuel for the stove. But like all young bloods he itched to have some coins in his pocket for the few frivolities that came his way on his one free day each week.

He had come to hate the witless drudgery of the daily plod up the hill from Dewsbury to Ossett when he knew the miners' strike meant there was no work at the end of it. He had dreaded the hours of standing around waiting for something, anything, to happen and knowing that to absent himself would attract the barbs and insults his mates reserved for the scabs who kept working throughout the strike.

Winter was well with them before Sarah's optimistic prediction eventually came true and Joseph gained a much-needed lift from the settlement of the dispute. Now that it was all over he felt there was once more a purpose to the day. He could almost enjoy being locked in the cage that slowly descended into the murky, dusty, cramped tunnels hundreds of metres beneath the moorlands. It was better to bend his back and wrench his shoulders for hours on end hacking out lumps of the black fuel than be huddled in groups outside the mine gates waiting for something, anything, to happen.

He was at last once again getting a regular wage – and even though the battle for an increase had been lost, his pay packet was still well above that of the average labourer. After months of enforced scrimping Joseph was not only contributing to the family budget, but also putting a bit aside for himself each week.

And so, over the ensuing years, life took its inevitable course. Sarah, who had begun her working life as a 14-year-old trainee nurse, soon followed the rest of her family into the mills where she spent several years as a rag sorter before readily accepting Joseph's halting but sincere offer of marriage. Her father, Michael Kelly, a rag grinder and a migrant from Ireland, had no hesitation in agreeing to the match; it would be one less mouth to feed.

The two families gathered in St John's Church, Dewsbury Moor, on June 5, 1897, when the vicar, the Rev W C Daniel, conducted a marriage ceremony for Joseph and Sarah that grafted the Kelly branch on to the Newsome family tree.

The newlyweds found accommodation in Kent Street, that same hillside warren of narrow streets, cobbled alleys and back-to-back cottages that had long housed near and distant relatives on both sides of the family.

It was an existence of incessant bone-chilling damp in winter and fetid airless rooms in summer, with poor sanitation and endless overcrowding. The simple luxury of a room to themselves was something no one living here would ever know. Little wonder that not a sign of them remains today; all were obliterated in the 1950s in what was appropriately labelled a slum clearance program.

Inevitably, it was not long before Sarah announced she was pregnant.

'That's reet good news,' said Joseph at this confirmation of his manhood. 'Our ma will be reet pleased too.'

Sarah stoically accepted this somewhat oblique greeting of her pregnancy; she was, after all, doing nothing less than what was required of her. In addition to all their other duties, wives were expected to procreate early and frequently, even though the clothing and feeding of a production line of offspring created an incessant strain on a family's meagre resources.

This first pregnancy ended in 1899 when son Harold was pushed out into the world with the help of Sarah's own mother, Joseph's mother and a couple of neighbours renowned for their midwifery skills. And so began a brood that reached a count of nine in a mere 15 years. This included Herbert who, in January 1901 and at the age of only 11 months, suddenly succumbed to the convulsions brought on by dentition, and four births – all boys – in the five years from 1901 to 1905.

With so many mouths to feed Joseph was grateful for the steady work that came with the rapid expansion of the Ossett coalfield. In terms of experience and knowledge, he was now one of the old hands and had progressed to the role of hewer – the man who actually digs out the coal.

'You make the shaft and I'll dig it out,' he would tell the strapping young men making their first anxious descents deep beneath the moors. The young bloods flexed their muscles in a show of unfelt bravado as the wires slowly unwound and their two-decker cage shook and rattled on its 'thimbles'. They wondered how much use such a small man could be when this was a job where brute strength was surely everything.

More than three hundred metres below ground they got their answer. No matter how thin the seam or small the space, short nuggetty Joseph would be squeezing in – rarely able to stand upright, often on hands and knees – to loosen and hack the coal from its bed.

In the early days, he and his mates worked on the butty system. This meant that, as the leading man, Joseph would negotiate a price with the manager or owner for removing coal and be paid by the owners. He then paid out his team based on his assessment of each man's value to their haul. Negotiated wages and union-agreed pay rates ended this arbitrary system and no one regretted its passing except those who abused their position of power and acted more like standover men than team leaders.

The Chidswell pit where Joseph began his mining days had been owned for more than twenty years by Crawshaw and Warburton Ltd, a growing company headed by local man Charles Crawshaw. As more shafts were sunk, the company gained a new lease of life with the owners consolidating their four mines under the name of Shaw Cross Colliery, thus pinpointing its location in the Ossett coalfield.

Throughout the turbulent period of dispute, strikes and eventual settlement the ownership and management remained steadfast, with Mr G F Blacher as manager at all four pits and Peter Winstanley as his undermanager. Both were loyal and long-term employees with Winstanley eventually becoming colliery manager. Between them they were responsible for more than six hundred below-ground workers, one of them Winstanley's own son, Bernard, and another hundred at the surface.

Great-uncle Joseph was among the 248 underground workers at the Shaw Cross pit. He and groups of his mates would cram into one of the steel cages that transported them into the murky and dusty world below. As the cage passed through cross seams, it would pause while men unlocked the gates and moved out into the widest part of the tunnel where trucks waited to be filled with the results of their digging and hacking.

'Another seam being opened up,' remarked Joseph as they neared pit bottom.

'Never stops,' said his mate alongside.

'Ay, but it's not us who's getting the money,' grumbled another. 'Ye should see t'place where Charlie Crawshaw lives. Up there on't Oxford Road. Just 'im and his missus and a daughter who's not done a day's work. Three of 'em, and they've got a live-in cook and two bloody servants.'

He got no response. It was a frequent complaint – a statement of the obvious; the gap between employer and worker was a chasm that showed little sign of narrowing.

Down on the pit floor the men lit their Davy lamps and handed them to the waiting deputy. He did a rapid safety check of each man's lamp, locked it and returned it to the owner before showing him where he would be working that day.

With their pick in one hand and their lamp in the other the men bowed their heads and bent their backs to enter the seam, its roof barely a metre high. Now almost doubled over from the waist they shuffled forward anything up to five hundred metres, feet wide apart, eyes fixed firmly ahead until they reached their designated worksite.

And so Joseph removed his jacket and shirt and began another six hour shift of bruising physical labour in an incredibly confined space where each blow of his pick sent another spray of dust and grit over his body, into his eyes and down into his lungs. He started by kirving, or hewing out about eight centimetres of the lower part of the coal face, to undermine it. Next he worked upwards on either side of this first cut in a process called nicking to prise out what is labelled as small coal. Wedges driven into the rock face, or gunpowder, were then used to displace what remained. When the dust had settled, he bent his back still further to shovel the lumps of coal into waiting tubs. And when that was done he started over, kirving and nicking and hewing at the next patch of coal in the wall in front of him.

Despite frequent disputes and stop-works – usually over pay, even at times succumbing to lower rates because of the fluctuating price of coal – Joseph was earning better money than the above ground workers. This meant he and Sarah were able to contemplate moving out of their cramped quarters in Boothroyd Lane, a narrow alley off Kent Street down the hill in Dewsbury, and migrating upwards, geographically if not socially, to be much closer to the mine.

'Think on it, Sarah,' said Joseph. 'I'd na have t'leave so early. And there'd be no more walking up't bloody long hill to Ossett.'

'Aye, and I'd be the one doing the walking if I'm to keep me job at the mill.'

For once, her body was free of any internal stirrings from a nascent child and she was working whenever she could at her old trade of rag sorter, the children packed off to school or left in the care of neighbours. The job meant a precious few extra shillings and, despite its tedious and physical routine, it was an escape from household drudgery and a chance for chatter and gossip with the other women.

'There's work up at Ossett,' countered Joseph. 'And we'd be up close to the moors; a bit of countryside for the lads to play in.'

'Hah, you call that countryside?' scoffed Sarah. 'You'd be lucky to find it through all the smoke and muck from the mines.'

Her arguments stayed strong until the day Joseph came home with a spring in his step and announced he had some bad news.

'They're cutting my wage,' he said, his back turned to her as he hung up his coat. He heard her sudden intake of breath and sensed her sinking down on to one of the wooden kitchen chairs. He turned to face her, unable to stop a smile flickering at the corner of his mouth. Sarah was drooped over the table, head in hands. She looked at him, perplexed.

'So what's to smile about?'

He couldn't contain himself any longer. The smile broadened into a big grin.

'There'll be less money but we're getting a house. Two rooms, maybe three, perhaps a garden. We can grow things for food. And the mine'll send us a fother of small coals every fortnight.'

He could hardly contain his excitement. Sarah was too stunned to respond, caught out by his jokey way of breaking his news; from bad to good in seconds. It all sounded too good to be true. His spate of words slowly convinced her.

'Think on it, lass. More space, close to work, better for the bairns and a fother of coal's about a ton and we can have it for only sixpence a load.'

'But why, Jo, why?'

'Because I'm a hewer. Right there at the coal face. The union keeps fighting for new deals all the time. That's why we have stop-works and strikes, to make the bosses see what we're worth. Where would they be without the hewers?'

Sarah at last caught her husband's mood. She pushed back her chair and stood and hugged him.

'You're a good man, Joseph Newsome.'

His news was more welcome than he knew. She gave him another hug.

'Perhaps it's just as well we're to move.' She patted her stomach. 'There's another bairn on the way.'

And so the Newsomes packed up their meagre possessions and said farewell to friends and neighbours in Boothroyd Lane. They trundled their way by horse and cart up the long winding incline of Wakefield Road, past the Heath Lodge Hotel that provided Lynne and I with accommodation a hundred years later, down the dip and up another hill to the township of Ossett to their new abode at Providence Buildings in Owl Lane.

The next child arrived and to their great delight it was their first daughter. Newcomer Annie took her place in the pecking order behind Harold, Stanley, Herman and Conroy but less than two years later had to forgo her role as the babe of the family with the advent of Harry, followed a mere year later by Elsie and then Lily and Eric.

Britain was now at war and young men were succumbing to the call for volunteers to 'do their bit'. Despite its importance to the war effort, mining was not a protected industry and it lost many of its workers to military service. It was a great relief to Sarah that Joseph was beyond enlistment age and that Harold, who celebrated his fifteenth birthday as war broke out, was the only one of their children at risk of facing the enemy if hostilities dragged on.

It was already getting too close to comfort. The German navy bombarded the Yorkshire coast only three months after war broke out, shelling Scarborough and Whitby on December 16, 1914. Six months later, on June 6, 1915, 24 people were killed and 40 injured when a Zeppelin let loose its bombs over Hull. And there were said to be already five thousand German prisoners of war camped not all that far away at Hipswell, in the North Riding.

Sarah had seen the recruitment posters that had been pasted up after the raid on Scarborough and prayed young Harold wouldn't do what so many others of his age were doing and advance his birth date by a couple of years so he could answer the posters' call and march off to war.

War or no war, Joseph stoically followed his routine of alternating foreshift and back-shift, one week working from four in the morning until ten, and the next week signing on from ten until four.

In the early hours of December 16, 1915, the day that Douglas Haig replaced the incompetent Sir John French as commander in chief of the British Expeditionary Force and Albert Einstein published his general theory of relativity, Joseph awoke as usual, roused by the sharp knock on his door by the "caller" doing his rounds. Sarah was already up, feeding baby Eric.

Joseph wasted little time in getting dressed in his thick white flannel pit clothes of loose jacket, vest and knee breeches. He pulled on long stockings and strong heavy shoes, and encased his head in a close fitting, thick leather cap. Sarah pushed a chunk of bread and a mug of water towards him. He chewed on the bread and gulped down the water; it was all he wanted at the start of a shift. Several of his mates preferred to have nothing.

He gathered up a tin bottle full of tea, another hunk of bread, his Davy lamp and a "baccy-box" and thrust them all in a leather pouch slung across one shoulder.

'Reet lass, I'll be off.'

With a light squeeze on Sarah's shoulder, a quick peck on her cheek and a gentle pat on the head for Eric, he was across the room and hurrying out the door to where Bill Farrar, his mate from a few doors away up Owl Lane, was already waiting.

'Reet booger of a day agin,' said Bill.

'Aye jest like yesterday and the day before and tomorrow and the rest of 'em,' grunted Joseph. 'Nowt changes.'

Bill chuckled.

'Aye, ya reet there, our Joseph. Nowt changes but leastwise we're not stuck in those trenches in France.'

'We've got our own trenches to worry about,' said Joseph. 'There's too many being killed in't pits w'out worrying about what's happening in France.'

Bill grunted in agreement and they scurried on through the dark and drizzle towards the looming pithead.

There was no warning; no preliminary slip or noise. As Bill Farrar later explained, the roof in the Beeston seam simply collapsed. His mate, Joseph Newsome, who had been sitting with his back to the coal face while Bill filled a tub, was buried beneath it.

Bill yelled for help. Others had heard the fall. They crawled and scrabbled their way forward as best they could through the rock and dust. Bill shovelled and scraped frantically, grime caking the sweat streaming down his back. It took ten minutes, but it seemed like an hour, to extricate Joseph from under the pile of fallen rock. It had knocked out only six pit props and was no more than a couple of metres long. Anywhere else along the seam and no one would have been hurt.

Joseph was dragged and then carried along the tunnel to the main shaft and the cage that wound him up the surface. His agony was clearly evident; his body was cut and bruised and he drifted in and out of consciousness.

A lad was sent with an urgent message to his home and a distraught Sarah rushed to the pithead, bending over the stretcher, clutching her husband's hands as he was laid in the ambulance that hurried them down Wakefield Road to the Dewsbury Infirmary in Moorlands Road.

Doctor Robert Beattie, a mature man of medicine, originally from Ireland but long settled in Dewsbury and married to a Yorkshire woman, did what he could to ease Joseph's pain but knew it was a thankless task.

The miner was too severely concussed. His head had taken the brunt of the fall. There were severe injuries to his spine and his left arm and elbow were badly damaged. The shock was too much for his system to cope. Doctor Beattie ordered doses of morphine to ease the pain and did what he could to repair the wounds.

Sarah knew from the look on his face and the way he spoke, that there was little hope. She stayed by his side as often as she could. Joseph's mother, Elizabeth, was there too, watching over her son as he went in and out of consciousness, barely coherent and unable to cloak his pain.

It was a bleak and mournful Christmas for all of them, with little joy for the nine children waiting at home for news of their father. Eventually, Joseph gave up his fight and died on Wednesday December 29 at the early age of 41.

The inquest, held two days later at the infirmary, heard that Joseph was a careful miner. The mine's deputy manager, George Crowther, told the coroner he had never found fault with any of his work. He also said he, Crowther, had inspected the site where the fall occurred less than an hour before and had rapped to roof with his hammer. He thought it was "all right". Later inspection had shown there had been a "slip" running from a pot-hole to the gate near the coal face.

Mr Crowther told the coroner he thought extra weight on the roof had caused the slip. No one contested his evidence. It was, decided Coroner Pelham Page Maitland, an unfortunate accident.

This was little consolation to Sarah, who told the court she had a family of nine to feed and clothe, of who only two were wage-earners.

'And both those are on lads' pay,' she added, as if to emphasise her plight.

She knew there would be little her relatives could do to help. Joseph's parents were now in their sixties and almost as impoverished as she was with Joseph's father Jonathan, my great-grandfather, eking out a living as a scavenger at the mills

A SHODDY LIFE FOR ALL

MY grandfather, Herbert Newsome, lived a lie all his life but I doubt that he knew it. If he did, he never let on. For as long as I can remember we celebrated his birthday on the eighteenth of September. One of those family anecdotal oddities repeated ad nauseam was that Herbert, known to me as Gramp, his daughter (my mother) and his grandson had birthdays exactly one week apart in successive weeks in September – on the fourth, the eleventh and the eighteenth.

It was only when I delved into our family history, long after mum and Gramp had died, that I found he and I actually shared the same birthday – the now infamous eleventh of September when, in 2001, the Twin Towers of New York came tumbling down. It was on that date in 1885, at 79 Middle Road in the Yorkshire wool-milling town of Dewsbury, that 32-year-old Elizabeth Frances Newsome pushed Herbert out into the world as the fifth child of what would finally become a brood of eight – four boys and four girls.

The father was 34-year-old Jonathan Newsome, the lad who had seen his own millworker father die a horrible death and was now plying the same trade as a wool dyer. He was too illiterate to sign his own name on the form registering his son's birth and had to make do with putting his 'mark'. From the time of their marriage in the autumn of 1871 Jonathan managed to keep wife Elizabeth almost continually pregnant. Hardly had one child been born than another was on its way. Only after giving birth to Harold at the age of 42 did she throw up her arms in exasperation and fatigue and announce 'That's it. No more'.

By then the Dewsbury they lived in had become an incredibly prosperous English town. Rapid development during the Industrial Revolution had transformed it into one of the global centres for the 'shoddy' industry – the recycling of old woollen items by mixing them with new wool and making them into heavy blankets and uniforms. The need to transport raw materials in to the mills and send the finished products out brought canals to the town in 1770, followed by the railway in 1848.

The town's woollen mills provided employment not only for Jonathan and his children but also for most of his and Elizabeth's siblings as well as the parents on both sides of the family and their siblings. Only Herbert's eldest brother, Joseph, had the misfortune to spend his working days in Dewsbury's other main industry – deep underground in the dangerous world of coal-mining.

Today, a third of Dewsbury's population of 60,000 come from southern Asia. They live in what has become, according to some colourful reporting, 'the town that dare not speak its name'. Newspapers say it is a byword for everything that is bad about Britain – the Dewsbury bomber, the Moslem veil row, the toddler who nearly died after being strung up from a tree, a man crucified ... and, most recently, the horror of the Shannon Matthews murder saga.

This once intensely proud Yorkshire community, with roots dating to 627 AD when St Paulinus founded a Christian settlement on the banks of the River Calder, is now a place that outsiders shudder at the thought of living in, or even visiting. A local barman was quoted in the newspapers as stating: 'I'm ashamed to say I'm from Dewsbury. Now, I say I'm from Leeds instead. It's horrible living here'.

It's a view supported by one of the several distant cousins discovered as I delved into my past. 'It's an awful place; that's why we moved away,' wrote one soon after we made contact and confirmed our common familial threads.

In Gramp's time, Dewsbury would have exemplified all that is seen as true Yorkshire grit – populated by solid, dependable working class people and an upper echelon of no-nonsense bosses, each dependent upon the other and trading mutual respect. 'Where there's muck there's brass,' was a truism recognised and honoured by both sides – and one that I heard Gramp repeat many times without any sign of rancour towards his bosses.

He made his first appearance in the Census in 1891, where he was listed as a five-year-old scholar. This is a huge exaggeration if we interpret the word as it is used today. Gramp was no scholar. He merely went to school, probably at one of the charity schools or free schools where the 3Rs of reading writing and 'rithmetic formed the mainstay of the lessons. And such schooling as he did receive ended soon after he entered his teens.

By the time of the 1901 Census, at the age of 15, he was already registered as an apprentice in one of Dewsbury's woollen mills, working as a piecer and scavenger. To reach apprentice status he had survived several years of child labour at its most arduous, first as a part-timer after school hours and then for the entire 12-hour working day.

'Just think yerself lucky,' his father Jonathan frequently reminded him. 'There was a time when there weren't no limit to the hours you had to work.'

Those were the days before the supposedly enlightened Factory Health and Morals Act of 1802 decreed that working hours for children in the mills should not exceed more than twelve a day. Subsequent legislation gradually eased the harsh conditions endured by mill workers but their work never ceased to be anything but relentlessly painful and dangerous, often resulting in life-shortening disease and injury.

Because the work of a piecer required considerable agility and dexterity the factories employed the youngest children, some merely six-years-old, for this physically demanding task. It was work that left piecers bruised, bleeding and barely able to walk at the end of their twelve-hour stints.

They spent their working days leaning over the spinning-machine to repair the broken threads, gathering twenty or more at a time, rubbing them together and then feeding them back to the spinner. A blow-by-blow account of a piecer's work has been preserved in *A Narrative of William Dodd: A Factory Cripple (1841)*. This tells the story of one young child who possibly suffered these hardships alongside my great-grandfather and his father before him. William Dodd provides a detailed description of a piecer's work:

> *Each piecing requires three or four rubs, over a space of three or four inches; and the continual friction of the hand in rubbing the piecing upon the coarse wrapper wears off the skin, and causes the finger to bleed. The position in which the piecer stands to his work is with the right foot forward, and his right side facing the frame: the motion he makes in going along in front of the frame, for the purpose of piecing, is neither forwards or backwards, but in a sliding direction, constantly keeping his right side towards the frame. In this position he continues during the day, with his hands, feet, and eyes constantly in motion. It will be easily seen, that the chief weight of his body rests upon his right knee, which is almost always the first joint to give way.*

A piecer could walk thirty or more kilometres a day. Little wonder, therefore, that William Dodd also recalls:

> *I have frequently worked at the frame till I could scarcely get home, and in this state have been stopped by people in the streets who noticed me shuffling along, and advised me to work no more in the factories; but I was not my own master. During the day, I frequently counted the clock, and calculated how many hours I had still to remain at work; my evenings were spent in preparing for the following day - in rubbing my knees, ankles, elbows, and wrists with oil, etc. I went to bed, to cry myself to sleep, and pray that the Lord would take me to himself before morning.*

Somehow grandfather Newsome not only survived his work as piecer with no perceptible permanent damage but also, thanks to the onerous demands of his apprenticeship, went on to learn a trade and eventually escape those 'dark satanic mills'. At some time between 1901 and 1911 this basically uneducated young man made the huge move to the south of England, reinvented himself as an electrician, found himself a wife and together they had their one and only child, my mother, Marjorie.

What such a proud and blunt Yorkshireman was doing even thinking of mixing with those softies from down south was something never revealed in my presence. You could take the man out of Yorkshire but never remove Yorkshire from the man. He gave little away emotionally. He retained the dour, stubborn gruffness of the breed, allied to a gentle earthy humour, right to the end: a stoic from the top of his flat cloth cap to the tips of his always shiny boots.

By the time he and Nan had settled into lower middle class prosperity at 86 Richmond Road, Gillingham, a terrace house now occupied by a firm of bricklayers, he had advanced his career to become a labourer and electrical wireman in His Majesty's Dockyard at Chatham.

In a nice touch of synchronicity of which he was totally unaware, this meant he was working alongside members of the other, paternal, side of the family who had rarely strayed from their long association with ships and shipyards. Thus there was a thread common to the lives of the Newsomes and the Berrys well before Marjorie met Bill and entwined the two families through marriage.

IN BED WITH LORD NELSON

TWO hundred and nine years to the day of its first opening we two cousins in search of our kinfolk checked into Milford Haven's Lord Nelson Hotel. Serendipity was with us; we were allocated the spacious first-floor Lord Nelson suite, complete with canopied four-poster bed and the view over the harbour that so inspired the future victor of the Battle of Trafalgar when he stayed there in August 1802.

As great-great-grandfather William John Berry reminded his son many times over, it was a day such as the still young town had never seen.

'It's what put this town on the map and made us what we are today,' he recited as he regularly reminisced about the day Britain's greatest naval hero honoured Milford with his presence.

'Everyone was there. They came from miles around. There were great crowds of us, out on Hamilton Terrace in front of the hotel, cheering and shouting fit to burst.'

William Berry was but a kid himself at the time, still in his teens and living up the road from Milford at Coombs. But he remembered the occasion well.

'There was Nelson up on the balcony giving his speech and such a crush down below. Everyone wanted to hear what he had to say. Such a speech it was, too. He reckoned he'd never seen a harbour like it other than some place called Trincomalee far away in Ceylon. And he knew all about the way the town took good care of the packet boats coming in from Ireland.'

William never ceased to remind his sons how Lord Nelson had heaped praise on the docking services, the importance of the wharfside Customs House and the role played by revenue men such as his second son, John (my great-uncle), who patrolled the treacherous coastline as a tidewaiter.

After this momentous event the hotel changed its name from the Star Inn to the one it bears today. But its imposing presence on Hamilton Terrace and its popularity with the locals remains as it ever was. One of those locals of a hundred and fifty years ago was grocer and merchant William Lloyd, brother of Lynne's great-great-grandmother and the confluence of our newfound relationship.

As we stepped out from the hotel into the crisp autumn afternoon each could sense the other's excitement as we counted down the numbers along Hamilton Terrace. Many of the buildings are little changed from when they were occupied by the town's movers and shakers, and money men, at the start of the 1800s. They are plain but solid, with little ornamentation, few balconies, doors opening right on to the footpath and their small windows facing out over the magnificent vastness of Milford Haven. Some still operate as the banks, guesthouses and doctors' rooms that they have always been. A few show signs of neglect and disuse; but most look neat and well cared for.

No explorer nearing the end of their quest has trod with more anticipation than Lynne and I as we passed the spick and span Barrallier House at number 24, with its sign proclaiming 'Built in 1797'. Only a few more metres to go. Number 25 was equally fresh and bright, although the iron grilles over its upper windows are jarring additions it could well do without. And there at number 27, on the corner of the road leading up the hill to Charles Street, a mere 400 metres from the Lord Nelson, stood the beautifully preserved three-storey house that was once the home of William Lloyd, his wife and their several children, one of whom left from this very house to marry my great-great-grandfather, Albert Jabez Berry.

'Our ancestral home,' we declared in voices tremulous with emotion and excitement. The thrill was akin to Livingstone discovering the headwaters of the Nile. Our individual tributaries ran off in diverse directions before this point but it was in this pastel painted merchant's home that the two lines first converged and our families had entwined.

We stood across the road among the clifftop flower beds and surveyed 'our house' like a couple of real estate agents planning a forthcoming auction. It was, in realtors' terms, a generously proportioned and well-preserved family home. Smaller windows up under the eaves of the slate tiled roof indicated attic rooms that once housed servants – a signpost to the Lloyds' prosperity and status. Apart from a fresh coat of paint, number 27 – in common with most of Hamilton Terrace – looked much as it would have done when first built at the start of the nineteenth century. Even its division into two apartments, one with a separate entrance in the side wall on Priory Street, has done nothing to mar its clean-cut lines. It is a heritage to cherish and one in which Lynne showed obvious delight.

Once again we were walking in our forebears' footsteps as she headed up the hill alongside 'our' house and into Charles Street, hailed in the local tourist guides as the town's 'traditional shopping centre' where the Lloyds were grocers, blacksmiths and general merchants. Now looking somewhat diminished and down at heel, the street was a thriving centre of commercial activity in William Lloyd's day. Although there is no business still bearing the Lloyd name, Lynne trembled with the certainty of one blessed with ESP and pointed to a double-fronted corner store.

'That's where they were,' she said. 'I know it. I can feel it'. She clung on to my arm, clasping tight, the frisson of feeling the past so palpable. Again, little was said as we walked slowly and pensively back to our lodgings at the Lord Nelson – a path assuredly taken so many times by our ancestors.

Our celebrations that night were as heartfelt as any that occurred when his lordship first put 'our' town on the map. But for the courtship of Alfred and Anne, we would not have been setting out on our own new-found relationship while quaffing good Welsh cider and tucking into a delectable meal of baked hake in a cockle and lava bread sauce.

SHIPBUILDERS AND WATCHERS

PAIN AND PENURY

IT was a terrible January day in the worker's cottage at the furthest end of the Welsh village of Coombs. It was the very depth of winter. It was numbingly cold and endlessly wet. Such roads as existed had long turned into quagmires. The packed mud floors of the cottage were scarcely much better. There were no floorboards. The chilling damp percolated into every corner. Rain seeped through the straw roof into the two rooms that housed John Berry, his wife and six children, four of them born in the past nine years.

And now another was on its way, without benefit of heating, running water or indoor sanitation. For Ann Berry, much as she was used to regular confinements, this must have been one of the worst. Why else would the church-going Ann tell John they would name the new arrival Jabez? She knew full well the name carried only one meaning: born in pain.

Its source was the line in Chronicles 4:9-10: 'his mother called his name Jabez, saying "because I bore him with sorrow".' Chronicles also says Jabez is 'a well-respected man and an ancestor in the lineage of the king's tribe of Judah whose prayer to God for blessing was answered.' and there was a brief period in the eighteenth and nineteenth centuries when the name's biblical connotations overruled its more negative side. However, it soon fell into disrepute and nowadays doesn't even figure on the list of the one thousand most popular names.

And so my great-grandfather, who gave his mother such a hard time in emerging from her womb on January 31, 1849, became one of the few children who have been burdened with the name of Jabez. Fortunately for him, his parents also preceded it with an Alfred. In the Berry family, this was the only time the Jabez label was used. But the Alfred tag lived on for two more generations.

As Ann Berry held the newly-arrived Alfred Jabez she was surrounded by three-year-old Emma, five-year-old Elizabeth, eight-year-old Joseph, nine-year-old Edwin and twelve-year-old John. There was nowhere else for this brood to go other than outdoors in the cold and mire.

Only sixteen-year-old Douglas escaped the groans and screams, and the stern orders of a village midwife who had little patience with women who made such a fuss about nature's routine. He was absent plying his trade as an apprentice shipwright in the Pembroke Dockyard. It was more than his job and his future were worth to miss a day working for a master to whom he was rigorously bound for the next three years.

This was communal living at its most cramped. A report to one of several nineteenth century royal commissions described the ordinary cottage in south Wales at the time as

"a rectangular building about 20 feet by 12 (inside measurement) with walls of mud (clay and straw mixed) or stone about 8 feet high".

Thus John, Ann and their seven kids lived in a space about the size of the average display home lounge room. Privacy was an unknown pleasure for, as the royal commission noted:

"Running back from each side of the door for 6 or 8 feet, and almost as high as the door are partitions, often formed by the back of a box bed or chest of drawers, by means of which partitions the inside space is divided into two small rooms, in one of which is a wide fireplace surmounted by a conical chimney."

Another account, written in 1814, described these squalid cottages as having *"a mud walling of about 5 feet high, a hipped end, low roofing of straw with a wattle and daub chimney, kept together with hay rope bandages, and frequently from its inclined posture making a very obtuse angle with the gable end over which it hangs".*

Despite the heartbreaking squalor of these cottages where there was *"no ventilation except what enters through the doorway and passed out through the chimney"*, the women of the countryside were so conscientious that the commissioner added that *"except in the north of England and in Scotland, I never saw such a general endeavour to make a poor building look its best"*, and this was despite the fact that many women worked in the fields throughout the day.

This Tudor-era type of cottage persisted in south Wales for at least two hundred years and when change did eventually come it usually consisted of little more than stone walling, the insertion of one or two tiny unopenable windows and the provision of privies.

There was little protection from winter's incessant rain – *"The mud cottage is almost always covered with straw thatch"* – and almost no natural light to dispel the gloom – *"In the middle of the front wall is the door with a small window on each side".*

A Reverend William Owen told the commissioners:

"The whole interior is open to the roof, except where boards or wattled hurdles are stuck across the heads of the walls to support children's beds. The floor is usually of mud or puddled clay. The only outside office is the pigsty, generally built against the end of the cottage. Such is a description of probably four-fifths of the labourers' cottages in the districts I visited".

And this was in 1867, almost twenty years on from the day Alfred Jabez was born; indicating little progress was made in improving the lot of the labouring classes. By then, however, the Berry family – with yet another addition, George in 1851 – had managed to move on to more substantial premises.

They transported their meagre goods and chattels little more than a mile down the road from the hamlet of Coombs – where they were registered in the 1851 Census as living at 'the last house'– to the medieval parish of Steynton and took up slightly more substantial premises at 71 Robert Street.

Steynton, then one of the largest villages in Pembrokeshire, has long since been subsumed by the one-time boom town of Milford which, in turn declined when its dockyard was moved across the sound to Pater and Pembroke after enduring years of grandiose plans that came to nothing. Robert Street remains as one of the main thoroughfares – a long straight that begins with a residential strip, passes through a depressed retail sector and ends in parking lots and a few more houses, among them the former Berry home at No 71.

When the family first moved there, Steynton (as it then was) had already been recognised by commentators as a reasonably fashionable parish and with somewhat more advanced living quarters. This assessment was mainly due to the fact that many of its houses had lofts, which were regarded as one of the characteristic innovations of the age. Some also boasted the luxury of individual privies, even if they were still outside.

Even forty years or so before my great-great-grandparents made their move, it was recorded that two of the five houses at Steynton consisted of four rooms on the ground level and a loft. That's the good news. The bad news is that these seemingly spacious homes housed as many as eleven couples.

The barns at the two local farmsteads accommodated six couples, a further six couples bunked down in sheepcotes and "chambers" adjoining the local bake-houses were home to eight couples.

The inclusion of lofts in Steynton's dwellings was about the only thing that set it apart from neighbouring communities. Housing in the district was otherwise virtually identical in design and the living conditions were just as cramped. A mile and a half down the road, at medieval St Ishmael's, three of the seven houses contained six couples. Two of these had identical outhouses with a barn for three couples, a sheepcote for five more and an outhouse housing four. Two of the remaining farmhouses were home to twelve couples.

Five generations on and the descendants of these Welsh dormitory dwellers have well and truly moved on. They have joined the ranks of the upwardly mobile that are scarcely out of their teens before they start demanding grants and financial favours to help them buy monstrous McMansions complete with home theatres, games rooms and triple car garages.

In the Steynton of today, which is now merged into Milford, little has changed. Any signs of prosperity have long passed it by. Its main street, where several of my relatives once lived, is no longer a thriving shopping centre but a sad succession of discount stores, low-cost supermarkets, boarded-up windows and empty shops desperately seeking tenants.

On Hamilton Terrace the parade of once rather grand and substantial homes still boast a panoramic view of the harbour but the buildings themselves are now mostly boarding houses, bank premises, legal offices and surgeries for dentists and doctors. Their view these days also embraces an expansive marina which, although crammed with expensive craft, is rimmed by a cluster of modern apartments, shops and cafes adorned, when we were there, by a profusion of To Let signs.

And down the hill at the far end there remains the magnificent bluestone building that was once the Milford Customs House built by Charles Greville in the 1790s as he tried to transform this backwater of farms and creeks into a bustling international seaport. Today it houses the excellent Milford Museum. But back in the mid-nineteenth century this was where my 2x great-grandfather, William John Berry, served his time as a tidewaiter – the forerunner of the career that my father, William's great-grandson, followed more than a century later.

It was an eerie and emotionally disturbing feeling to push open the solid timber door into this weather-worn maritime relic and to know we were treading the same thick floorboards as were once walked by our ancestors. How strange to be ducking beneath the same low beams while running hands over the thick stone walls that protected them from the gales and rain beating in across the sound. The ghosts were abroad.

Even weirder to think that among William's colleagues was Peter William Blair, Lynne's great-great-grandfather who, in 1855, married Margaret Lloyd, sister to William Lloyd, Lynne's 2x great-grandfather.

Peter, a Scot born in Greenock, Renfrewshire, on September 30, 1832, five months after the April 10 wedding of his parents, had served time as a boiler maker's apprentice in Greenock before joining the coastguard service. He was transferred to Milford in the early 1850s and was working as a boatman.

It was a small community, built almost entirely around the harbour and its activities, so there is little doubt that William (was it shortened to Bill, as was my father's name?) and Peter knew one another and had many a chat on the dockside or in the pub.

There was even more synchronicity in realising that this centuries' old building was almost identical to their counterparts all around Cornwall's rugged coast where I went as a lad accompanying my father –William Berry's Customs officer great-grandson – on his rounds. It resonated with the past. It spoke to me so strongly that I felt I could almost reach out and take from great-great-grandfather's hands a mug of sugary sweet tea that was surely as much the staple winter warmer of these guardians of our coast in his time as it was when Dad and I dropped into Customs Houses from Falmouth to Fowey and from Padstow to Penzance.

For a precious brief moment the gap between generations ceased to exist. We had come together with our ancestors in a weather-beaten bluestone building on a windy harbourside in Wales.

WATCHERS BY MOONLIGHT

IT was a crisp wintery night. The headlands and inlets around the wide expanse of Milford Haven's harbour were clearly etched by a moon occasionally hidden by a light veil of scudding clouds. A cluster of seagoing boats rocked gently at anchor in the mainstream, safe from the huge swells of the nearby Atlantic Ocean.

Suddenly, there was a fresh rippling of the water close to the shoreline. Something had disturbed the calm surface. Keen ears could hear the faint sound of oars squeaking in their rowlocks. A skiff rowed by two men emerged from the shadows. The men leaned back and gave a final thrust of their oars to push their craft up on to the pebbled beach.

As they stepped warily on to shore, heaving a bundled load between them, there were shouts from further along. Lanterns threw a shaky light on the scene as two other men emerged from hiding behind a low brick wall. There was confusion, a confrontation. The flash and explosive crack of the powder from a gun being fired shattered the quiet. The boatmen sprinted off. The men with lanterns attempted a half-hearted chase but soon gave up and returned to inspect the bundled package. They took a furtive look around. After a whispered discussion, they hauled the abandoned cargo up the beach and into the shadows.

A cloud drifted across the moon. All was darkness and quiet once more.

The following morning, William Berry, my great-great-grandfather, sat with wife Ann at the kitchen table in their cramped two-roomed cottage as he told her about the incident on the beach the night before. Theirs was the last house in the village of Coombs, straggling along a wooded hillside bordering Pill Creek, a few kilometres inland from the harbour

'They were too quick for us,' he said.

His wife gave a dismissive sniff and wiped a cloth over the rough wooden table.

'Just as well, I'd say. I don't want you coming home cut to pieces by some ne'er do well. Don't know why you ever took that job on. You wouldn't be the first to come home covered in blood or worse.'

William felt it best not to answer. His decision to throw in his job as a joiner and join the Customs service was a running sore between them. It seemed like a good idea at the time when he weighed up the seeming security of a government job against the haphazard shifts available in the fledgling dockyard.

Ann, however, was deeply concerned about the dangers of his new career. But there were other issues that disturbed her. She would rather have her husband coming home bone-tired and weary from a long shift in the dockyard than have people in the village turn away when she approached. Tidewaiters would never win a popularity poll. They ranked low on the public acceptance scale and this attitude flowed through to their wives and families. Locals saw little harm in the smugglers' activities; most regarded them as social benefactors when they made essentials such as salt and tallow readily available for a third of the price demanded by storekeepers.

'You'll never win,' said Ann. 'Almost everyone's against you.'

Again, he knew she was right. There were too many stories told in the hotels and on the wharves of otherwise upright citizens who thought nothing of siding with the smugglers rather than supporting the government's law enforcers.

'Look at that Mr Raymond,' chided Ann. 'Supposed to be so law-abiding.'

William knew the story well. Justice Raymond meted out penalties on local lawbreakers 25 kilometres away around the coast at Solva on the shores of St Brides Bay. When a villager decided to chalk up a few brownie points by informing him of the imminent arrival of a cargo of contraband salt, the justice put on a wonderful show of storming down to the harbour. He bellowed his anger as he went, his voice guaranteed loud enough to warn everyone in the area. By the time he had been ferried out to the allegedly offending vessel there was not a skerrick of salt to be found on board. It was now part of the local folklore that the waters of Solva Harbour were somewhat saltier than usual the next day. Nor was anyone hauled before Justice Raymond to face charges of smuggling.

William allowed himself a flicker of a smile at the thought.

'It's not funny,' reprimanded Ann, now in full flight on her favourite hobby horse. 'No one was hurt that time. But look what happened over at Pen-y-bont Bridge. I don't want you coming home on a stretcher.' She paused. 'Or worse.'

William knew she had a point and was well aware of the incident even though it had occurred more than a day's walk away from his own territory. It was one of the worst of many cases in which the smugglers had shown scant regard for the armed force of the law. A notorious local smuggler by the name of Jolly was leading a team of drovers moving contraband from the shores of Cardigan Bay through to England when they were confronted by the revenue men at Pen-y-bont Bridge. What was described as 'a bloody battle' ensued with dead and dying bodies left behind as the smugglers fled into the hills.

In other similar incidents it was often the Customs men who, although armed, came off second best. Only a few years before William Berry joined the service the Pembroke community was shocked and divided by the violence that ended the 'reign' of 'the king of the smugglers', a charismatic local character named William Truscott. This well-known organiser of smuggling rings throughout south Wales was eventually captured at New Quay in one of the caves used along Cardigan Bay for storing smuggled goods. He managed to escape (or was there connivance at his release?) and fled all the way to Pembroke, some 80 kilometres away.

Customs men caught up with him as he was trying to cross the Pembroke River and opened fire. Truscott was hit and wounded. The Customs men claimed the smuggler drowned before anyone could reach him but bystanders alleged the officers ignored his cries for help. An inquest jury agreed and found the revenue officers' action was 'highly reprehensible, cowardly and cruel'. They were never going to win.

William Berry's job title of tidewaiter (or wayter) is one that no longer exists although it aptly defined his daily duty. In today's parlance he was a Customs officer who waited for the high tide to bring in the ships. More importantly, he waited for the smugglers who were making use of these ships, either as crew or by ferrying in goods to their coastal hideouts. The entire Pembrokeshire coastline had a long history as a favoured haunt of smugglers, who tended to be more supported than condemned by all levels of society.

William's task was to board the incoming vessels and check that they dropped anchor at the appointed place in the harbour, making sure the cargo was not unloaded on an isolated jetty out of sight of the waiting controller, collector and surveyor (all no doubt eyeing each other suspiciously). The tidewaiter, too, was under observation – from a tide surveyor.

According to *The Letter-Book of John Byrd, Customs Collector of South East Wales 1648-80* (edited by S.K. Roberts), a waiter (wayter) or tidewaiter was a job low on the rungs of the civil service ladder. Nonetheless great-great-grandfather William would have needed to be sufficiently literate and numerate to pass the Civil Service examination for tidewaiters. It was a test which would have stretched the abilities of many of today's students, who are so deeply dependent upon their pocket calculators and spellcheckers.

William not only had to prove he could write, but also that he was able to write clearly, with correct spelling and an understanding of a word's current usage. The examination also posed several questions to test his arithmetic – or maths, as it is known today. *A Guide to the Civil Service Examinations,* compiled by P. S. King in 1856, asked would-be tidewaiters to divide 59,436,784,379 by 492 and wanted to know how many square inches there were in 50 acres. Or how about calculating the number of loads of hewn timber in 2,160,000 cubic inches? Those taking the exam had to add columns of money, weights, volume and length. Tests of subtraction, multiplication (978,015,632 by 9,738) and division (95,708,654 by 298) completed their ordeal.

The twin forces of land-based Customs officers and coastal patrol boats became the basis for the country's war on smuggling that continues to the present day. In William Berry's time, however, their effectiveness varied greatly according to the calibre of the officers, their pay and conditions, and other factors. When pay was good, and the service was able to hire committed and diligent officers who could call on the military for assistance, the preventive effort could be remarkably effective.

Sadly, this happy state seemed to exist for only a minority of the time. For example, the riding officers who patrolled much of the coast were not only poorly paid but also had to dip into their £42 annual salary to buy and maintain their horses. Little wonder that even a small denomination banknote was enough to see a blind eye turned when a contraband run was on.

Corruption and disloyalty were not limited to the lawmakers and there was little joy for those who tried to do the right thing. Ann Berry well remembered as a child hearing the story doing the rounds of a woman who found that her husband had stowed a cargo of smuggled French brandy in the cellar of their Swanlake home.

The woman decided to make a quick (and secret) two hundred pounds for herself by informing the Customs officers and collecting a reward. Unfortunately, she couldn't resist telling her plan to a friend who then told the woman's husband. The smuggler quickly rounded up his mates and the barrels of booze were well on their way to happy buyers when the Customs men arrived to face an empty cellar.

The scene of this incident was within walking distance of the magnificent spread of Manorbier Castle, an off-the-beaten track treasure harking back to Norman times and which was at the centre of the nineteenth century smuggling trade. It was here that a larger than life character named Captain Jack Furze conned the locals into letting him take over the lease of the farm attached to the castle.

He spun a yarn about having saved some money from his seafaring days and that he would now devote his energies to running the farm and digging for coal while still doing a bit of coastal trading in his brig, the *Jane*. The locals soon discovered the coastal trading was more to do with illicit barrels of brandy than anything else and the digging was more to create tunnels for escape and storage than to prospect for coal.

Manorbier Castle remained a hotbed of smuggling activity until Jolly Jack's little boat was fired on and almost run down by a Royal Navy ship. The cruiser crushed the decking of the *Jane* and pursued it relentlessly until nightfall forced it to call off the chase. The incident convinced Captain Furze he'd had enough danger and he opted for a quieter life. Two centuries later, the smugglers' tunnels still honeycomb the ground beneath Manorbier Castle as testimony to the extent of the captain's thriving illegal trade. However, they are unlikely to be trod by their modern counterparts with their far more sophisticated methods and much bigger fish to fry.

The fact that the navy had crushed Jolly Jack's boat and set the man on a more legal path did little to comfort Ann Berry. Such victories were few for the law enforcers and the danger they faced was too great. Smugglers had been known to ram the Customs patrol boats, even to board them and attack the officers, forcing them to flee and leave their boat to be scuttled.

Ann pulled out a chair and sat at the table opposite her husband. She reached for his hand and covered it with hers. She kept her voice low, no longer hectoring.

'I know you meant well, a steady job, maybe promotion and not so hard on the body,' she said. 'But it's too dangerous.'

William looked at her. He could feel her concern.

'Look at last night,' his wife said. 'You said there was shooting. You could have been killed. I get so worried. And there's the children …'

Her voice trailed off. She was determined not to nag. Yet she was at her wits' end; and so weary with eight children and still in her thirties. But there were other aspects of being married to a tidewaiter. As Ann was well aware, the problems were exacerbated by the fact that the officers lived in the heart of the communities they were supposed to be policing. If they were diligent in their efforts to prevent smuggling, they were ostracised and persecuted; the alternative was collaboration with the smugglers, an easy life, and a regular supplement to the meagre pay. It was an easy option that helped the coasts of Wales, and also Cornwall, become happy hunting grounds for the likes of Jolly, Furze and Truscott.

Little wonder, therefore, that great-great-grandfather Berry had second thoughts about his mid-life career change. Egged on by wife Ann, he eventually returned to the skilled trade of shipwright that was followed by the men of the family for three generations until my own father cancelled his dockyard apprenticeship … to become a Customs officer.

William Berry never allowed his sons to suffer the mistakes of their father. His instructions were definite.

'You'll be apprenticed to a good master and learn a decent trade,' he sternly told them as they reached employable age. His dogma was 'don't do as I do but do as I say.'

He had learnt a hard lesson when he did what was so rarely done in those days and switched trades, making his move from joiner to tidewaiter.

'It's not so hard on the body,' he told wife Anne as they discussed his decision. 'And the money is no worse. It will be more secure, too, working for the government.'

Secure, maybe, and also physically less demanding than hauling and fixing the timbers used in building the dockyard's growing fleet of ships.

But, as he soon discovered, the hours were terrible and the constant exposure to an unfriendly climate even worse. As the job title implied, a tidewaiter's duty hours were governed not by the clock but by the incoming waters. He, and the ships he had to check, waited for the tide to be high before their work could proceed. It was a job for all hours and all weathers.

He quickly came to realise the monotony and hard labour of a shipwright's daily toil were the lesser evils. And he made sure his sons knew it. One by one they were apprenticed off, signing the onerous indentures that would rule the first three years of their working lives.

Eighty years later, William's great-grandson, my father, Wilfred Berry, echoed his actions by forsaking life as a shipwright (as had been his father and grandfather before him) and took the civil service examination to become a member of HM Customs, those latter day successors to the tidewaiters of the 1840s.

A LONG-STANDING CUSTOM

IT IS the early 1950s and I am a teenager standing on a Cornish cliff top. A gale is blowing in from the same Atlantic that has forever also stormed into my ancestral home along the Welsh coast at Milford Haven. It is an intensely black and moonless night, much as it was when smugglers used the dark to evade the watching tidewaiters four generations ago. Our faces are stung by needles of icy rain as we seek shelter in the lee of a hand-built stone wall. There are few lights to be seen in the solid stone cottages of the fishing village clinging to the slopes either side of the narrow harbour down below.

We hear the putt-putt of a two-stroke engine somewhere along the rutted, winding track. The beam of a headlight cuts through the darkness, showing the shards of rain are almost horizontal. The motor-cycle slows to a crawl and turns into the lay-by where our car is parked. My father, the chief preventive officer for Cornwall, steps forward and greets the motor-cyclist.

'Evening, Les.'

'Evening, sir. They'll all be indoors tonight.'

Dad agreed. This was not the weather to be tempting the tide and running a small boat into the narrow treacherous coves below. He took the logbook Les had removed from his pannier bag. He checked the schedule, made pretence of looking at his wrist watch and appended his signature. All was well; no matter the weather or the time of day, the men of HM Customs were guarding this inhospitable coastline on foot, pushbike and motor-cycle.

Sadly my father was never aware of the synchronicity; that he was a direct descendant of one of the first men to have defended the British coast against illegal imports. There's no doubt that had he known he would have displayed his officer's commission with even greater pride.

This document, now hanging framed on my office wall, states

> *'He hath the power to enter into any ship, bottom boat or other vessel and also in the daytime with a writ of assistance and taking with him a constable or other public officer ... to enter into any house, shop, cellar, warehouse or other place whatsoever within any port or place whatsoever there to make diligent search and in any case of resistance to break open any door, trunk, chest or any package whatsoever for any uncustomed or prohibited goods and the same to seize ...'*

And so it goes on – the flowery bureaucratic language of the early nineteenth century empowering a public servant of the late twentieth century. It seems such an antiquated system to have persisted unchanged into the age of airport body searches, drug lords and international arms smugglers – so olde-worlde and reminiscent of *Masterman Ready*, the *Boy's Own Paper* and the tales of Daphne Du Maurier, a writer who lived and wrote little more than a sailor's curse from where we stood on that storm-tossed night.

Work as a Customs officer has been a job opportunity for career-minded young Englishmen for more than 800 years. And the basic job description has changed little since 1275 when Edward I brought in a tax on wool exports to put some much-needed cash into the nation's coffers.

It became a lucrative source of income that soared after the Black Death plague of 1349 reduced the population of England from about 4 million to 2.5 million in little more than a year. Landowners looking for a less labour-intensive form of agriculture found it in sheep-farming. Land that had been open to all was ditched and hedged and herds of sheep began grazing where serfs had once sweated. Wool production rose dramatically and, with it, the potential tax revenue to the crown.

With taxation there inevitably came tax avoidance and the king recruited the first Customs staff to oversee the system. At first, the small full-time force of Customs officers concentrated on collecting the revenue: they had neither the time nor the resources to ensure everyone paid up. It was when the court realised a considerable amount of evasion was occurring that the Customs officers became enforcers as well as collectors – a dual role that remains unchanged today.

The monarchs that followed Edward found more and more goods to tax – wine was next after wool – and devised numerous ways to increase the levies. Instead of taxing goods at the source – on the farm, in the mills or warehouses – it was easier to enforce duties and penalties at the places of import and export. Britain's island nature made sure of that. With its borders clearly defined by the sea, shipping movements were relatively easy to detect. Sailing times for square-rigged ships depended on wind, weather and the rise and fall of the tide. At low water, boats simply grounded in the mud at the foot of the quay. Trade along the coast was easy to spot.

When Edward I created the Customs service, he provided a custom house with a small staff at thirteen officially designated points around the coast. To land goods at any other port needed permission from the authorities at one of these main ports. This meant Customs officers not only had to handle ships entering the official ports but also to maintain a watch over the entire coastline in between. In East Anglia, for example, the Customs officers at Yarmouth had to keep watch on 140 kilometres of coastline, north to Blakeney and south down to Woodbridge.

Responsibility for levying the duty rested with a collector of customs, the man who actually did the work, and his boss, the controller of customs. The two men were supposed to collect the dues payable, and sign and seal the relevant receipts and other export documents. As a precaution against dishonesty the port seal was made in two halves with each official holding a half. All documents had to carry both halves to be legal, and each official was separately accountable for the port's transactions.

Customs officers were poorly paid and the precautions did little to stop them profiting from seizures of smuggled goods or making a charge on every receipt they sealed. They put their seal to blank receipts that a merchant simply filled in with whatever figures suited him. Blank receipts were so commonplace by 1433 that a penalty of three years jail plus seizure of all belongings was introduced.

Towards the end of the seventeenth century wool exports from England's southern counties got seriously out of control with an estimated 120,000 packs of wool being exported illegally each year. In the southeastern county of Kent, my birthplace, wool exporters, known as 'owlers', became so determined to evade government levies that hundreds of armed men were eventually involved in each owling venture.

In a bid to stop the rot, Charles II set up the Board of Customs in 1671. By 1685 there were ten smacks patrolling the coast between Yarmouth and Bristol. In 1690, what was described as a force of mounted Customs officers – called riding officers – was established. This was something of a misnomer as the 'force' expected to patrol the entire Kent coastline consisted of a mere eight riding officers.

The riding officers not only had to contend with the owlers, but with the growing tide of smuggled imports. The most recent war with the French had necessitated a further hoisting of import duties and smugglers found they could now make a profit on both legs of their cross-channel journey. Ships that went out loaded with wool came back groaning with foreign luxuries.

The inadequacy of manpower among the riding officers in Kent was recognised in 1698 when the force (now called the landguard) was expanded, at first to 50 and later to 300. And so the concept of a land-based patrol became well established. But the upper hand remained with the sea-borne smugglers who could simply land goods at the point where the preventive effort was weakest. It was left to the navy to oppose the smugglers at sea until, at the turn of the century, a fleet of 21 Customs boats (the current Waterguard) was stationed all around the coast to intercept and board ships before they made landfall.

To stop rising corruption and enforce honesty, a surveyor of customs was appointed at each port to monitor controllers and collectors. As the number of dues increased the service expanded and more officers were introduced.

To thwart the unscheduled offloading of goods, Customs officers began boarding ships down river or well before they neared their anchorage. In London, for example, the tidewaiter joined boats downstream at Greenwich to make sure the cargo was not unloaded on an isolated jetty out of sight of the waiting triumvirate of controller, collector and surveyor (all no doubt eyeing each other suspiciously). The honesty of the tidewaiter was ensured by the presence of yet another official, the tide surveyor. And so another bureaucracy was born.

Once a ship had been guided into dock, other officials took over. A coast-waiter supervised the unloading of cargoes from home ports while a land-waiter watched over loading and unloading of boats from foreign ports. A land surveyor kept an eye on both of them. Languishing at the bottom of the Customs ladder was another trio of officials: a man called a searcher checked that the ship's cargo tallied with what was on the receipt; a weigher unpacked the cargo and weighed it; and a tidesman stayed with the vessel until the unloading was complete. Such men were my ancestors along the coast of Wales.

The cliff-top patrolmen whose schedules Dad checked in Cornwall's coves, bays and remote fishing villages also lived in their communities like our ancestors did in south Wales. But the smugglers these days came from without, not within. The stakes were higher, the goods more dangerous and the people involved ran their operations by phone and telex from anonymous big city offices. And now the internet and mobile phones have upped the stakes even higher.

The patrols, regardless of how quaint and antiquated they might have appeared, were as effective as when first introduced by King Charles three hundred years earlier. Those intending to glide seemingly innocently into Cornwall's coves and harbours doubtless paid scant attention to a man on a pushbike pedalling gently along the cliff-tops. Yet few carriers of contraband escaped those keen eyes. Details of any craft seen cruising out of the main shipping lanes soon had its details transmitted up the line and a boarding party was waiting on the quayside when it eventually made landfall. At other times action was more immediate with the Customs cutter coming alongside way out at sea and team of eager dungaree-clad searchers clambering aboard ready to crawl into every corner and crevice to ferret out illicit goods.

Dad relished such moments. It was *Boy's Own Adventure* stuff to him – a man who was forever younger than his years. There was nothing he loved more than getting out from behind his desk and its mounds of bureaucratic paperwork and heading out across Falmouth Bay in the teeth of a gale to clamber up a meagre rope ladder swaying and banging against the side of some suspect ship.

Occasionally, against all the rules and in a way that could never happen in today's over-regulated society, he secreted me aboard the Customs launch to let me share the thrill of the chase – great moments of father-son bonding with a man who remained forever young.

SHIPWRIGHTS AND WRONGS

IT was all Admiral Lord Nelson's fault. If Nelson had not tried to flatter the locals when he descended on south Wales in the summer of 1802, my great-grandfather, Alfred Jabez Berry, would probably not have trundled his wife all the way up to Scotland in the 1870s and brought her all the way back again little more than ten years later and by that time with three children in tow.

Likewise, many others in our family may never have left the shores of Milford Haven and my roots would still be firmly entrenched in ancient Welsh soil rather than having been transplanted to shipyards and ports throughout Britain.

Largely because of a throwaway line from his lordship, grandiose plans by landowners and misguided policies from a ramshackle Admiralty led to Milford Haven going through a period of boom and bust in which the lives of hundreds of local people were turned completely upside down. And the Berrys were among them.

It seems likely that Alfred – responsible husband and breadwinner – made the migration north simply in search of work that had been brought to the Milford waterfront by Nelson and his followers, and then almost as quickly snatched away through lack of planning and foresight.

There has been much debate and doubt about what Lord Nelson actually said in a speech in Milford Haven on August 1, 1802. However, it is generally accepted that he heaped excessive and unjustifiable praise on the local harbour which, until then, had mainly provided a sheltered anchorage from Atlantic gales, a landing point for ferries from Ireland

and a base for a small but eventually unsuccessful whaling venture run by Massachussetts imigrants. From there, things began spinning badly out of control.

Maybe the great naval warrior was carried away by the occasion - a dinner given in his honour on the anniversary of the Battle of the Nile. Or perhaps he was merely keeping in the good books of his mistress, Lady 'my dearest Emma' Hamilton, whose husband, Sir William Hamilton, owned land on the north shore of the Haven that his family was planning to develop as a town and shipyard.

The land, close to the village of Hubberston, was administered by Sir William's nephew and heir, the Hon Charles Grenville, whose mistress Emma had been before he 'passed her on' to his uncle. Joining Emma, her husband William and nephew Charles at the dinner table, the emotional Lord Nelson got somewhat carried away by the company, the grandeur of the occasion and the adulation of the local gentry.

The party had already detoured to Merthyr Tydfil where two correspondents travelling with them arranged for a large crowd to lead a procession to Nelson's lodgings at the Star Inn where he was greeted by a banner painted with the words 'NELSON AND NAVY' and a band playing *Rule Britannia*.

Nelson waved from his hotel window and accepted three hearty cheers from the crowd. Local ironmaster Richard Crawshay was so excited by the visit that he invited Nelson to tour his works at Cyfarthfa. There he grabbed Nelson by the hand and shouted words to the crowd that were widely reported and entered into the folklore of the visit: 'Here's Nelson, boys; shout, you beggars!' A party was held later at the Star Inn where Nelson's health was toasted with Welsh wine thought to have been supplied by another ironmaster, a Mr Homfrey of Pendarren.

Everyone was after Nelson's patronage and attention, especially those who saw a sleepy hollow being turned into something much more lucrative. It is little wonder that in his dinner speech in Milford at what has since become (not surprisingly) the Lord Nelson Hotel, the admiral did what was expected of all keynote speakers on such occasions and made a flattering remark to his hosts. Although the actual words have never been verified, he is quoted as saying something along the lines of the waters around Milford being 'one of the finest possible stations for the British Fleet, with command of a safe and capacious anchorage for the entire navy'.

He was clearly telling his audience what they wanted to hear and perhaps trying to give a boost to his friends' failing shipyard. His remarks, however, had a much greater effect than he probably ever intended upon the history of the Haven and its connection with the Royal Navy. They also underscored Nelson's own ambition to play a greater role in how the navy was run and the ships that it built.

The much-feted admiral was, however, further off course than any of his fighting ships had ever been blown. The Haven had almost none of the requirements for what he seemed to be suggesting. It lacked flat land with deep water close to the shore. Also, because there were no local oak forests, the timber to build the ships would still have to come from the Baltic – and Milford was further from there than any other shipyard in Britain.

The area was mainly rural and lightly populated. Skilled labour was almost non-existent apart from men who had worked at a small shipyard at Neyland on the Haven's north shore and a small community of Quaker whaling families from Massachusetts who had settled around Hubberston. In addition, the lessees of the Hamiltons' shipyard had already gone bankrupt without a ship being completed and had seen their yard taken over by the Navy Board on a yearly lease. All in all, the Haven was not a bright proposition, Nelson or no Nelson.

But reason takes a holiday when bureaucrats scrap among themselves and wars are being fought between nations. Distant decision-makers followed Nelson's lead and decreed that the waters of Milford Haven were a shipbuilder's dream. Dockyards were built at Pembroke and a community of farmers and landed gentry, with its roots in the land since medieval times, turned to new trades such as shipwrights, carpenters, joiners, riveters and tidewaiters.

Although the harbour was less than ideal for Nelson's grand plans, the Berry family were among those who accepted the opportunities these great changes appeared to offer. They were able to prosper in a way not open to previous generations. They acquired skills that would guarantee employment throughout their lifetimes and were able to move from squalid village life into more substantial accommodation. They became upwardly mobile in a slow but steady working class sort of way.

From very humble homes built along the creekside in the tiny community of Coombs – a place today obliterated by thickly treed woodlands and no longer on any map – they graduated to terraced homes in the growing townships of Steynton and Milford Haven. Later they crossed the harbour to small but solid single-storey houses built along the hillsides of Pennar overlooking Pembroke Dock and the broad expanses of the Haven.

Great-great-grandfather William set a pattern that was followed down the generations when he took up the tools of a joiner and, after a short dalliance as a tidewaiter, progressed into cabinet-making. Most of his sons did likewise, and their sons, too, as they endured the rigorous years of apprenticeship to become workers of wood as shipwrights and carpenters. Their homes – whether in Wales or elsewhere around the British Isles – were always within siren sound of a dockyard.

The tradition only died out when my father, Wilfred Berkeley Berry, defied his master shipwright father by turning his back on a dockyard apprenticeship. But, fittingly, he did so to assume the mantle of a Customs officer which, as already recounted, was the same role played by great-great-granddad William when, as a tidewaiter, he patrolled the creeks and estuaries of Milford Haven in search of smugglers and their contraband.

And so the wheel turns full circle ...

THE LONG MOVE NORTH

TO great-grandfather Alfred Jabez Berry there was only one solution. But breaking the news to wife Annie was not going to be easy. He took his time walking up the slope from the ferry to the family home on Marine Terrace; he needed to think and to plan his words.

He needn't have bothered. She knew all was not well the moment he pushed open the door and bent his head beneath the low lintel. His movements were too slow and tentative and the look on his grimy, weather-beaten face did little to dispel any doubts. Her first fears were that there had been accident; someone else they knew had been maimed, even killed, as they laboured on the slipway. It happened too often. There was so little protection for men sawing, chopping, carving and planing too close together in such confined space. Sharp tools, relentless deadlines and demanding bosses were a fatal mix.

She gave him no chance to compose his words. Not even waiting for him to sit on the kitchen chair and unlace his heavy boots.

'What's happened? What's wrong?'

He shrugged, almost relieved he didn't have to pussyfoot around deciding what to say.

'There's no work. We've got to move.'

There, he'd said it. No long explanations.

'What do you mean, move?'

'There's work up in Scotland. On the Clyde.'

'Scotland!'

It was unthinkable. Unimaginable. Near neighbour England was a foreign country. Scotland was beyond foreign; a place Annie had heard about but of which she knew next to nothing. Her family, the Lloyds, had lived here for generations. Alfred's family was the same. Except for Annie's uncle, David Lloyd (Margaret and William's brother), who emigrated to the USA, none had ever ventured more than a few miles in any direction. She and Alfred had gone to the same school; their families lived only a few houses apart. And now he expected her to pack everything up and move far away from all she had ever known.

'What's wrong with staying here?' she asked. 'This is our home. Everyone we know is here, not hundreds of miles away in Scotland. Anyway, where would we live?'

'Seems they're so desperate for workers that they're building homes for them to live in. And right close to the docks, too. It's the only way, love; there'll be no work here soon and we can't live on nothing.'

Annie knew the truth of everything her husband was saying; but it was not what she wanted to hear. It was little more than a year since he had walked her down the aisle after their wedding at the parish church at Steynton and they had yet to start a family. This, however, was more than likely to change, and fairly soon too if past events were anything to go by. She was one of six children and Alfred was one of ten. Big families were the norm, despite the high number of deaths in childbirth and infancy.

'But things will change,' she argued. 'They have before.'

Alfred shrugged, wanting to share her optimism but knowing what the talk was like down on the docks. Most of Pembroke depended in one way or another on the dockyard but the decisions on how it was run were made far away in London by the Lords Commissioners of the Admiralty. They had regularly been petitioned by the locals to let Pembroke fit out ships completely rather than merely build the hulls. But their lordships steadfastly ignored these pleas, just as they refused to heed calls for a receiving ship to be based at Pembroke. Such vessels were stationed at naval bases to handle and train recruits and would thus be a boost to the local economy. It had been a precarious see-sawing existence for the people of Pembroke Dockyard ever since Lord Nelson encouraged the port's expansion and none were more aware of this than the men who laboured in its sheds and slipways.

Alfred's father had quit his trade as a joiner for several years in uncertain times and had returned when the orders for ships once more flooded in. He had then encouraged his sons to follow him and most were now out of their apprenticeships and fully-fledged joiners, shipwrights and carpenters, skilled in working with the heavy timbers used for the hulls of the navy's ships.

'Things are changing,' said Alfred. 'We're in the wrong trade.'

Annie frowned. His words made no sense. Her husband had done his time as apprentice, learned his trade and was an essential part of what Pembroke did best – build ships. How could he be in the wrong trade?

'We work with wood, not iron.' Alfred spread his hands wide. 'It's as simple as that. They're saying there'll soon be no more timber ships.'

'Who's saying? People spreading rumours, I'll warrant. Haven't you anything better to do than listen to lots of idle gossip?'

She was fired up and angry, irked by the seriousness of her husband's demeanour, how he seemed to have really thought about things before making his announcement. She was in shock at the thought of leaving friends and family.

Alfred put a comforting arm around her shoulder.

'I'm sorry, Annie, but it's all true. The first iron warship has already been launched, the *Warrior*, up at Blackwall on the Thames.'

'Hah, an iron ship,' she scoffed. 'How do they expect it to float?'

'Just like a wooden one,' he said. 'And it's tougher, won't catch fire so easily or be damaged by gunfire.'

The evolution of the iron warship had left the Admiralty facing a number of problems. Suddenly almost every major warship in service had become obsolete. France was already building a series of ironclads (timber ships sheathed with iron armour). It was the emergence of these ships, plus a shaky relationship between the two countries, that had finally spurred the Admiralty to change to iron construction. *Warrior* and her sister ship, the *Black Prince*, being all iron, were superior to their French contemporaries but the British shipyards did not have the capacity to match the French programme 'keel for keel'. And so the Admiralty decided that the design of certain timber ships under construction should be modified drastically and be completed as ironclads. Three such vessels were built at Pembroke and on Thursday June 26, 1862, a Miss Jones of Pantglasl, described as "a Carmarthenshire lady" performed the ceremony when the yard launched its first iron-cased warship, the *Prince Consort*. She was followed by three more interim ironclads, the *Research,* the *Zealous* and the *Lord Clyde*.

The frigate *Lord Clyde,* launched on October 13, 1864, and her sister ship, the *Lord Warden,* were truly massive vessels for those times. The main shell of the hull was twenty-four inches of timber bound by one and a half inches of iron, then a six inch thickness of planking. On top of that was armour five and a half inches thick and finally round the waterline a four inch belt of oak.

While these hybrids were being completed the Admiralty was considering the future of Pembroke Dockyard and what it found did not look promising. The yard was not well suited for building the ships of the new era. There was a small coal field nearby but it produced anthracite, not good steam coal. Iron works were far distant. The numerous slipways built in earlier years for seasoning the timber hulls were no longer an asset. Pembroke, once the most modern of shipyards, was becoming as obsolescent as the ships it had proudly built.

Elsewhere in the country there were already commercial shipyards skilled in working with the new material; they were usually adjacent to coalfields, ironworks and engine builders, often all belonging to the same company or ironmaster. Pembroke shipwrights such as the men of the

Berry family did not know much about iron, and probably did not want to know.

As they and their fellow shipwrights and carpenters worked on *Lord Clyde* they feared it would be the last, or almost the last, wooden capital ship to be built.

'Better make it a good one,' William Berry said to his sons. 'Give them something to remember us by.'

'Not so sure about that,' said eldest son Douglas. 'It's more like a wake than something we should be celebrating.'

His brother, John, agreed.

'I'll do as good a job as ever but I can't say I can get up much enthusiasm. Where's the pride in having all your work hidden by sheets of iron? My heart's not in it.'

Alfred had said nothing but listened intently to his father and his brothers. He was newly apprenticed to the dockyard and bound by strict terms of employment that allowed no scope for dissent or opinions. Nonetheless he could not help but wonder what the future held. Where was the sense in learning all the skills needed to work with timber when the future seemed to be one of hammering metal rivets and bending sheets of iron? Even if the future of the yard was less gloomy than his brothers were predicting it was obvious there would be much less need for workers in wood.

No sooner had the *Lord Clyde* been launched than the word went around the yard that the Government was considering closing the royal dockyards at Deptford, Woolwich, Sheerness and Pembroke. The radical proposal was given strength by reports that the *Lord Clyde* was proving to be something of a disaster. Not only were her main engines very unsatisfactory (which was no fault of the Pembroke shipwrights) but her performance was being adversely affected by the use of large quantities of insufficiently seasoned timber caused by the Admiralty's rush to use up stocks. Nicknamed the Queen's Bad Bargain, she was soon suffering from a rotting hull and within

10 years was sold for scrap.

The Government eventually decided to reprieve the Pembroke and Sheerness yards and close only Deptford and Woolwich, making Pembroke the second royal dockyard, after Chatham, to be equipped for building iron ships.

'I suppose it's better than nothing,' commented William Berry.

'At least we've still got jobs,' countered Douglas. 'Not like those poor devils in Deptford and Woolwich.'

'I hear many of them are being transferred down here, so the navy must think there's going to be enough work for them as well as us,' said John.

William lapsed into moody silence. All these changes were hard to accept. In little more than a lifetime Pembroke shipbuilding had seen sail gave way to steam and screw propellers replace paddlewheels. Now wood was being overtaken by iron and, eventually, steel. He hated the clamour, fumes and ugly foundries that now infested the yard. The open slipways where timber was seasoned were being closed in under high roofs because iron, if left exposed to the elements, would soon rust. William was a craftsman who relished the scent of oak and pine and the gradual shaping of a length of timber beneath his plane or adze. He looked at Alfred.

'You're the new breed, son. You're going to have to learn new skills. You'll be working with metal instead of wood. But it won't be the same. Iron doesn't speak to you like a piece of wood does.'

Alfred remembered these words now as he confronted Annie. He understood what his father meant about the way a piece of wood could be moulded and shaped but he also feared for his future if he didn't adapt to the rapid changes taking place around them. He was a young man with responsibilities: only two years married, he had a wife to provide for and already Annie had hinted she intended they would soon have other mouths to feed.

'We've got to look to the future,' he urged her. 'Everything's so uncertain here. Work is slowing up. The bosses are making changes but it's taking too long. There's work a-plenty up on the Clyde and the bosses are building homes for their workers.'

Annie could see his mind was made up and admitted to herself there was solid sense in much of what he had said.

'OK,' she said, but without showing too much enthusiasm. 'If you think it's for the best, that's what we'll do. Just promise me we'll come back if it doesn't work out or if things pick up here.'

Alfred willingly promised. It was what he had already decided they would do. He had as little desire as Annie to leave Pembroke and the family and was determined they would return at the first practical opportunity. But for now, he was sure the Clyde was the place to be.

DEATH IN THE DOCKYARD

THE word spread quicker than the echo of a riveter's hammer in the dry dock. The four-storey tenements of the Linthouse Buildings resounded on Tuesday July 3, 1883, to frantic shouts and the pounding of boots on the stairs as the bringers of tragic news knocked on doors and yelled the sparse details.

'A ship's gone down,' was the terse message. They needed to say little more. The wives, mothers and children who rushed to their doors and gathered in the stairwells knew what it meant. They didn't require lengthy explanations; the urgency and brevity of the messengers' cries said it all. The commotion voiced their worst fears; the dread they lived with every day as their menfolk trudged off for another shift in the Glasgow shipyards.

Already there was a hurrying stream of people flowing towards the massive steel gates of the fortress-like premises of Alexander Stephen and Sons. They were stumbling and pushing, showing little regard for those around them despite their common panic. Everyone in that river of desperate people was focused on the fate of someone they cared about who was working behind those formidable red granite walls.

Ahead, sirens were wailing. Burly, official-looking men in black suits and bowler hats stood at the shipyard gates, trying to hold back the growing crush of people. Emergency carriages threaded their way in from the street, the horses steaming and twitchy, their drivers yelling to clear a path through the crowd.

A voice called out 'It's the *Daphne*'. Others took up the refrain. Cries of 'Oh my God' or simply someone's name greeted the news. They knew where their menfolk were working and their fears soared even higher. Others hugged themselves in silent relief at their good fortune or let out a gentle sigh at they drew their children closer, comforted by knowing their man was working on some other ship. This was not the time to display their joy at a loved one's escape.

More than two hundred miles away, in one of the many terraces of solid houses winding around the hillside above the Pembroke dockyards of south Wales, Alfred and Annie Berry sat in their kitchen table at 58 Military Road, Pennar, staring grim-faced at the newspaper spread out on the table before them. The big, bold headlines were frightening; the long columns of news below them even more so. The terse confronting words across the top of the page said it all - Shipyard disaster on Scotland's River Clyde. A hundred and twenty three dead. Many more maimed and injured.

'That's our shipyard,' said Alfred, his voice a tremulous mix of fear and anxiety. 'We could have been there.'

His finger traced down the list of the dead. So many familiar names.

'That could have been me,' he whispered.

Annie put a consoling hand on top of his. Even from this safe distance in terms of miles and time it seemed like a narrow escape. The news brought home the ever-present danger the dockyard workers faced in those days long before the words "workplace safety" had ever been paired and voiced. They leaned forward together as they read the roll call of the dead. The address of some of those killed – Linthouse Buildings – leapt out at them early in the list. There was a gasp from Annie.

'Oh look there's that young man from number 30, almost next door,' she said.

Her finger hovered over the name Daniel McKay, an apprentice fitter aged 18. 'And there's another,' she said, pointing to Angus McNab, a trainee engineer from number 14.

Further down were the names of more men Alfred had worked with or passed on the stairs on their way to and from work. There was William Duncan, 30, a carpenter, also from number 30 and James Hall, a joiner from number 18.

Others from Linthouse Buildings to lose their lives were labourer James Carbary, 22, apprentice fitter James Hutchison, 17, and labourer Peter Bradley, 32.

The list went on and on, a litany of tragedy that Alfred and Annie were all too well aware could have included Alfred's name. One victim's body remained unclaimed. The paper recorded that 'upon this body there were found a caulk-line, a gimlet, a two-foot rule, a pocket knife marked "W.H.", a pair of boot laces in pocket, three lead pencils etc.'

'Poor man,' said Annie. 'To die like that and then have no one to claim you or to bury you.'

They continued reading the newspaper in gloomy silence. Of the 200 workers on board the 460-tonne *Daphne* as she flipped over, 124 had died. At first, it had seemed like any of the hundreds of launches that took place up and down the Clyde. But because her owner, the Laird Line of Glasgow, was eager to have her finished for the Glasgow Fair holidays the *Daphne* had an unusually large number of workmen on board. Her engines were also placed on board before the launch, and her boilers were to have been installed immediately afterwards.

Shipbuilders worked largely by rule of thumb and past experience and had little knowledge of how to calculate the stability of their vessels. There were the usual two anchors and cables in place to steady the vessel after she entered the water. But, for some inexplicable reason, this checking apparatus failed to function. The starboard anchor moved some six or seven yards, but the port anchor dragged for about sixty yards. The current of the river caught the ship at a critical moment and, within just three minutes, had turned her over on her port side.

On reaching the water, the *Daphne* floated perfectly, then rolled over on her side and sank. Most of the men on board were trapped inside the holds, engine-rooms and cabins in which they had been working. As the ship toppled over, many on board were tumbled into the water. Men and boys who had been busily putting in the finishing touches were suddenly shrieking and yelling. Twenty or so managed to scramble on to the vessel's hull or cling on to its side. Instead of the cheers and hurrahs normal to such an occasion, the air was filled with the shrieks of drowning men.

The skippers of a flotilla of small boats that had been assisting at the launch rushed to the scene, gathering up the desperate survivors. Although divers were sent down immediately, they could do little to help. It was not until about ten days later that the vessel was partially moved, and almost three weeks before she was docked.

One survivor, a joiner named Kinnaird, was reported as saying that before the accident there were so many men and boys on deck that it was difficult to move about.

'I cannot possibly describe the heart-breaking scenes I witnessed,' he added.

'It must have been terrible,' said Annie. 'To think that …'

She let her words hang in the air, her thoughts needing no further expansion. It was not much more than a year ago that they had returned from Scotland and the lengthy report brought back so many memories. The move had not been as bad as she had first feared and she and Alfred had not only returned home to more prosperous times in the Pembroke dockyard but, to the delight of their parents, had also brought with them two sons and a daughter born on Scottish soil – one of them being my paternal grandfather, Alfred Berkeley Berry.

Things had turned out much as her husband had assured her they would. There was security of work as the Glasgow shipyards went through an incredible period of expansion and prosperity. A scarcity of labour meant wages soared and the workers were able to negotiate improvements in conditions. The housing, too, had been far better than she had at first feared.

Clydeside was booming. What had previously been a relatively insignificant shipbuilding industry in the 1820s had expanded rapidly as wood and sail gave way to iron and steam. Engines devised by local man David Napier were installed in the boats that plied the Clyde estuary and across the Irish Sea. While Australia boomed from the rush to gold, it was a rush to iron that saw the townships along the Clyde expand like never before.

In 1830, Napier's cousin, James, invented a boiler that reduced fuel consumption by some 30 per cent. His cousin, Robert, moved down river from Lancefield to Govan at the end of the 1830s and rapidly secured some of the contracts for Cunard's transatlantic steamers. Soon, men trained in the Napiers' yards went on to form new shipbuilding and marine-engine firms along the Clyde. By 1864 there were more than twenty shipyards and by 1870 more than half the British shipbuilding workforce was based on the Clyde, producing half of Britain's tonnage of shipping. Shipyards had workforces of a thousand or more and, in 1861, were paying carpenters thirty shillings a week. Joiners were getting from twenty-two to twenty-six shillings depending on the quality of their work and in 1864 secured a rise of three shillings, while the carpenters' pay was increased to thirty-six shillings. However, although 1865 opened with a whole year's work on hand, shipbuilding slackened off and carpenters suffered a pay cut of six shillings a week. Another surge followed, and the late 1860s and first few years of the 1870s brought the century's biggest boom. Workers flooded in from all over Britain, including Alfred with wife Annie in tow, who was still nursing fears of miserable living conditions.

In a fairly short span of time Govan had changed from being a sleepy waterside rural waterside hamlet favoured by landscape artists to become the fifth largest burgh in Scotland, earning a description as "the shipbuildingest burgh in the world."

In 1793 only 224 families lived there. Most were handloom weavers or dyers occupying single-storey thatched cottages. In the surrounding countryside were several extensive and prosperous farms whose owners lived in nearby large country houses. The area's several market gardens and the fields on Govan Moor were famous for the quality of their potatoes, turnips and other crops. Thirty years later the local mines were producing enough coal to fill three hundred trading vessels a year. And with the coming of the shipyards the thatched cottages in the "Auld Toon" and the country houses were demolished; in their place rose the first great blocks of sandstone tenements.

Soon there was hardly a soul crammed into the few square miles around Govan who did not depend on ships and shipbuilding. As a result, housing was intolerably cramped and sub-standard. The difficulties created by the rapid population growth had been noted as early as the 1820s and 1830s. Big open spaces and grand city squares were already being sold off for housing. Mansions that housed a single family were converted into tenements housing a dozen or more. By the 1840s some of the city's housing conditions were regarded as among the worst in Europe. Lethal outbreaks of cholera, typhoid and typhus found easy and regular targets among the overcrowded and the highly mobile population living in the foul 'backlands' and dingy lodging houses. Polluted water supplies, a smog-laden atmosphere and a lack of sunlight added to the inhabitants' health risks.

Supply lagged behind demand, leading to considerable overcrowding and all the social problems that accompany poor and cramped living conditions. By 1864 the population had risen to 9000 and Govan gained the status of a burgh. The influx continued and the 1891 census counted 61,500 residents within its boundaries. By 1912, there were 91,000 living there and all autonomy was lost.

Fortunately for Alfred and Annie shipyard owner Alexander Stephen was one of the more enlightened entrepreneurs who tried to do something to ease these shocking conditions. In 1869, he bought the 18-acre Linthouse estate to the west of Govan to build his shipyard and converted the old mansion, one of Govan's most impressive country houses, to serve as offices and later (during the First World War) as a canteen. The first ship was launched there in 1870 and the yard's engine and boiler works were completed the following year.

Alexander Stephen always had the welfare of his workers at heart. While overseeing the building of his shipyards, he also ordered the construction of houses at nearby Linthouse for 120 men and their families. Alfred and Annie eventually moved there – into number 34 Linthouse Buildings – after initially finding rooms nearby at 19 Logie Street, a link between Landlands Road and Elder Street that is no longer there.

If ever the much-abused expression 'a tight-knit community' was apt, it was here, among the tenement dwellers on the banks of the River Clyde in the late 1800s where almost everyone was a migrant enduring the daily struggles and challenges faced by newcomers the world over. Annie often felt alone and far from home and this was the sort of communal support she craved and relied on, especially when she felt the first stirrings in her belly of the couple's first child.

'What wouldn't I give for some fresh air and a bit of peace and quiet,' she moaned to Alfred as lay alongside him and tried to shut out the noise rising up the stairwell.

She appreciated that Govan offered plenty of work and good wages but there was no relief from the noise, smoke and overcrowding as the town became home to more and more heavy engineering plants, iron and steel manufacturing factories and to vast tidal docks and graving docks. It was a far cry from the life she and Alfred had left behind.

True, Pembroke had its docks, slipways and workshops but nothing on a scale such as this and in only a matter of minutes from home they could be among fields, headlands, hills and beaches along the magnificent Pembrokeshire coast where the air was fresh and clean … and thankfully remains so today, preserved as a superb national park.

Annie did her best to accept the conditions in Linthouse and soon had plenty to occupy her with the arrival of Alfred Berkeley, born at 10.50pm on October 3, 1875. Where the Berkeley comes from, no one knows. However, when Agness, Alfred's sister, gave birth in Milford a year later she also burdened her son, Thomas, with the Berkeley middle name. And it was extended into the next generation when Govan-born Alfred Berkeley Berry attached it to his son Wilfred, my father. Apart from these two instances it appears nowhere else on the many branches and twigs of the family tree.

As Annie strived to adapt to life in Govan she found her new role as a young mother helped her forge contacts and friendships among many of the other residents. Shared hardships and experiences brightened and eased the daily grind of tenement life. This was especially so when, well before Alfred Berkeley's first birthday, other women began noting her pallid look and regular bouts of sickness and asking if all was well. One of them gave her a friendly nudge.

'Looks as if there's another bairn on the way,' she commented with a smile.

'No doubt about it,' said another.

When they confirmed what Annie already suspected she happily broke the news to Alfred and at six o'clock on the morning of February 19, 1877, the couple welcomed the safe arrival of a boy they named Hugh.

It meant one more mouth to feed right at a time when the shipyards began facing a precarious future. There was considerable industrial friction in the yard, culminating in a six-month strike by carpenters which, despite their persistence, ended with no increase in wages for the workers.

Alfred could see uncertain times ahead and began wondering whether their move away from Milford had been such a good idea. It was a depressing thought and one he decided to keep to himself. Annie had enough to worry about ensuring their two boys stayed fed and healthy.

Down on the docks all the talk was of the competition the Glasgow yards were feeling from the ever-expanding Clydebank firms. Orders were declining and harder to win. There were fewer shifts available. With the introduction of steel hulls in the late 1870s, the shipbuilders needed to invest heavily in newer and more sophisticated equipment. That meant raising money, going into debt in a big way and cutting costs – and wages.

In 1874 the yard at Alexander Stephen was so busy that deliveries began to fall behind and several owners protested. Carpenters' wages were increased to eight pence an hour, but then, because of the increased costs, business began to decline. In April, one customer, the Hamburg Trans-Atlantic Company, was obliged to ask for credit; although this was granted, the company was forced at the end of the year to relinquish one of the vessels under construction.

For many firms, however, their fate was decided not from within the industry but by the sudden and disastrous collapse in 1878 of the City of Glasgow Bank. The bank's operations had already been suspended in November and December the previous year when a deficit had been discovered of something like £500,000 in today's terms. An agreement with other Scottish banks and the closure of its New York office enabled it to resume trading to the extent that in June 1878 it declared a 12 per cent dividend and claimed to have 133 branches and deposits of around £600 million at today's prices.

Suddenly, on October 2, the directors announced the bank's closure. It was bankrupt. Behind a facade of profit and responsibility were nett liabilities of more than £500 million. These had been brought about by poorly secured loans and a broad portfolio of speculative investments in Australasian farming, foreign mining stocks and American railway shares. Balance sheets and profit and loss statements had been falsified and the share price held up by secret purchases of the bank's own stock. So successful was its deception that on its last business day the bank's £100 shares were selling at £236.

The shockwaves spread far and wide. Scores of Glasgow businesses failed as a result of the bank's collapse. Many shipbuilding firms were among them. In the subsequent general economic recession orders for ships slumped dramatically. It was little consolation that the directors were arrested, found guilty in Edinburgh High Court and sentenced to terms of imprisonment.

Few were immune but some were hit less hard than others. Shipbuilder Andrew Stephen, whose workers lived in Linthouse Buildings, was among the latter but it still meant tougher times for Alfred and Annie and the seed being sown of thoughts of a return to Pembroke.

To help bolster their falling and uncertain income, Annie suggested taking in boarders.

'There's plenty of single men looking for somewhere to sleep,' she said.

Alfred greeted the idea with a puzzled look around their small flat.

'But where would they go?'

'We'll just have to squeeze up. The boys will have to sleep with us. We could do with the money and I'm sure it won't be for long.'

Alfred knew she was right – but was convinced her optimism was misplaced despite the boom or bust nature the shipbuilding industry had shown over the past century. The word down in the yard was that the boom times were well and truly over. Orders were scarce and it appeared that any recovery was going to be a long time coming. With such uncertainty, working hours varied considerably between the many shipyards. But although trade was somewhat slack, working hours on the Clyde were increased from 51 to 54 a week in order to give a faster turnaround on such work as did come in.

Annie put the word about and within next to no time welcomed two young single men as lodgers – cousins David Christie from Arbroath and William Christie from Methven, near Perth, both engine fitters in the nearby yard.

Undeterred by the bank collapse, Alexander Stephen maintained its high reputation for reliability and first-class vessels and was able to obtain better prices than many of its competitors. As work was about to begin on laying down some vessels for its own account it received an order for four ships from a new company to be known as the Clan Line and agreed to take shares in the venture. Its first ship, the *Clan Alpine*, was built at Linthouse and launched at the end of 1878. And when the line later experienced some difficulty in arranging finance, builder Stephen arranged for extended terms to tide the young company over until more prosperous times.

By the end of the year, Alfred's gloomy prediction was beginning to fade. Business had revived and Alexander Stephen had recorded the second highest output for the year among Clyde shipbuilders. The residents of Linthouse Buildings celebrated long and hard when they took their short break for the New Year holiday.

'I reckon we've earned this and more,' said Alfred as he shared a jug of ale brought from the pub by his young lodgers.

He got no argument from them but the bosses were more forthcoming. They claimed the men had worked much harder than usual in the week before Hogmanay in order to boost their pay packets. One voiced the opinion that 'If workmen would work all the year round as they did this week it would make a great deal of difference, both to themselves and to the yard'.

He probably had a point because although the yard entered 1880 with so many orders that it stopped tendering for new vessels, work did not advance as rapidly as might have been expected. Workers were becoming less compliant, stoppages and strikes were more frequent and productivity was not always as expected.

Alfred sensed the change in mood and remained anxious about the future. This wasn't helped by the cramped conditions at home and the lack of clean air and open spaces for Annie and their boys. Their only escape was to Elder Park, just around the corner from the tenements, but it was hardly what he considered an open space compared to the wild

Pembrokeshire coast.

Annie, too, was feeling the strain and often wondered about Alfred's promise that they would return to Pembroke if things didn't work out. She welcomed the extra money her lodgers paid each week, but was increasingly depressed by the irksome lack of living space. And once again there were stirrings from within her body as another child began to make its presence felt. She broke the news to Alfred and made her feelings known.

'I'd like to go home,' she said. 'You promised we would and this is no place to bring up children.'

He readily agreed and admitted he shared her longing to be back with their families in Pembroke.

'Perhaps you should write and let your folks know the news about the babe,' he suggested and wrapped an arm around her. He gave her a smile. 'And while you're at it maybe find out if there's work to be had for a shipwright who's worked on the Clyde.'

The relief was palpable. Their hidden thoughts and concerns were out in the open and there was little dispute about their future plans, even when Alfred suggested they delay their return to Wales until after the birth and even to wait past winter when travelling with three young children would be easier.

Elizabeth Emily was born in Linthouse Buildings at 10.20 on the morning of October 30, 1880. And although the Alexander Stephen shipyard began the following year with 31,000 tons of work on hand (rising in a few months to 40,000 tons) and carpenter's wages were increased to 31s 6d a week (equivalent to about £90, or £4680 a year, in today's purchasing power), Annie and Alfred stuck to their plans. They returned to the family home in Military Road, Pennar, where they spent the rest of their days in working class comfort as solid and respected members of the local community.

With them were the only Scottish-born members of the Berry family, one of whom – my grandfather, Alfred Berkeley – later took the brave step of crossing the border to find work in the dockyards in Chatham. His brothers also made similar moves to Devonport, Portsmouth, London and Coventry. And so began the English branch of a tree that for centuries had been deeply rooted in the soil of Wales.

Today there are merely seven Berrys listed in the Pembrokeshire phone book. Military Road, however, remains much as it would have appeared when this was the family home – a long undulating street of neat and well-kept homes leading out to a headland overlooking the sea and with views down the hillside to the docks and shipyard. Windows and doors have been modernised, the inevitable satellite dishes adorn the roofs and walls, and backyard and attic extensions have been subtly added. But the essential character remains of a solid working-class street with solid working-class values.

Little wonder that when great-grandfather Alfred Jabez Berry died suddenly here on March 22, 1929, at the age of 80, the *West Wales Guardian* recorded the death of "one of Pembroke Dock's oldest and most respected inhabitants". It reported his funeral at Llanion Cemetery was attended by "a large gathering of sympathisers, including many of the deceased's former dockyard colleagues".

The newspaper noted that Alfred was "a regular attendant and devoted member" of the Pennar Weslyan Church, of which he had been a trustee for many years.

His will granted probate and "all my real and personal property" to his youngest son, my grand-uncle Wilfred, and listed effects totalling £56 – roughly equivalent to a year's basic wage.

NOTE: At an enquiry into the sinking of the *Daphne* the yard owners were exonerated from any blame, leading to claims of a cover up. One outcome was to limit personnel aboard to only those necessary to moor the ship after the launch. The ship was raised and repaired at Govan Dry Docks and emerged as the *Rose*. Such was the scale and tragedy of the disaster that there are two SS *Daphne* memorials in Glasgow. One is in Elder Park, Govan, and the other on the other side of the Clyde in Victoria Park, Whiteinch, representing the loss to those communities involved.

SO THIS IS WHERE DAD WAS BORN ...

ALL praise to the town planners and developers of Plymouth – the solid Devonshire city that provided a greensward for Drake's pre-Armada game of bowls and farewelled the Pilgrim Fathers.

Amazingly, despite all the post-war rebuilding of this bomb-devastated port and today's large-scale reconstruction, they have so far allowed one of my family's homes to live on into the twenty-first century. The house in Devonport where my father was born still stands. But only just, I feel, and probably not for all that much longer. The changes that have taken place around it suggest the wreckers and developers cannot be far away.

This remnant of my ancestral links is an island of Victoriana surrounded by a valiant attempt at bringing a sense of community, lower crime rates, safety and some civic pride to an area once deemed to be seriously lacking in any such concepts. Known as Morice Town after a loyal supporter of King Charles II, this corner of Devonport had declined into a community divided by through routes and rat runs, with roads carrying traffic travelling at inappropriate speeds into and across Plymouth. It was riven by anti-social behaviour and a total lack of communal spirit. All this made it ideal to be selected as one of nine areas for a national Home Zones pilot scheme that ever so slowly overcame residents' apathy and suspicion.

By turning it into a jigsaw of narrowed streets, speed humps, no entries and limited access it reduced incidents of violence, theft and damage by more than 90 per cent, cut through-traffic by 40 per cent and stimulated the creation of community groups and events. The most visible testimony to the area's rejuvenation is the Morice Town Primary School, which is set in the centre of this maze and runs along the back fence of my ancestral home. In 2010, Morice Town Primary finished in the top 200 most improved primary schools in England and was number one in the Plymouth table.

For many frustrating moments it appeared as if the place I sought had, like the maternal grand-parental homes in Dewsbury, been razed into oblivion. There seemed to be only a loose correlation between the narrow streets we drove along and the maps downloaded from Google. Things got no clearer when we parked the car and paced out the supposed route.

Balfour Terrace seemed to have been developed out of existence during the city's massive urban renewal. And then, suddenly, there it was – with the street nameplate annoyingly affixed to a wall several metres in from the corner position where such signs are usually found. It was one of those Eureka moments that family historians cherish. Here, in this well-preserved and fairly imposing house, were my family roots. Such occasions set the spine a-tingling and curtail all need for speech.

Number 11 Balfour Terrace sits midway along a single row of solid two-storey Victorian houses. It is surrounded by a tight maze of low-rise mainly public housing that, despite the Home Zones regeneration, seems totally devoid of any hint of prosperity or cheer among its residents. A large Salvation Army depot and store at the end of the street is a clear indicator of the area's fortunes and misfortunes which, for so long, were firmly tied to the historic naval dockyard that sits a mere gentle amble away down the hill to the harbour. Even the local pub, The Albert, has an insubstantial and temporary look about it.

Standing there outside this old family home it occurred to me that we are what our ancestors made us. How else can I explain my peripatetic life – one that has kept me wandering restlessly for almost eight decades? Even now, in my seventy-sixth year, I flit on a whim between Australia and England still uncertain of where I should call home. This hither-thither component of my DNA can perhaps in part be traced back to great-grandfather Alfred Jabez Berry who moved wife and family from South Wales to Scotland over a period of ten years, during which time wife Anne gave birth to three children, one of whom was Alfred Berkeley Berry, outside whose house I now stood.

He did as his father did and criss-crossed the country – from Milford to London and on to Kent, then down to Devon before returning to Kent and several different homes. With such genes in my blood and a father who maintained the family trait for half a century is it any wonder I suffered an endless itch to be on the move and eventually adapted so readily to life as a travel writer?

Alfred Berkeley Berry moved to Balfour Terrace with wife Emma and baby son Alfred Sydney – always known simply as Syd – soon after the start of the twentieth century. They travelled close to 400 kilometres from another naval location, the Kent borough of Gillingham, where Alfred worked as a shipwright in the dockyard at Chatham – a brisk walk along Brompton Road from their home in Saxton Street.

This was at a time when the Chatham dockyard was stumbling through a turbulent period of great expansion and change. Suddenly the use of electricity became a recognised engineering skill and an entirely new set of trades opened up to the workforce.

By 1908 the installation of electric light and power was completed in all dockyards, allowing the permanent adoption of year round 48-hour working week. It also meant the dockyard had to reorganise to create construction, engineering and electrical engineering departments – trades totally foreign to born and bred shipwrights such as Alfred Berry. Little wonder, therefore, he accepted the opportunity to move elsewhere.

From the early 1800s Britain's naval dockyard workers were sent where required, even abroad. Sometimes this was because of a dockyard's expansion and at others it happened when the reduction of working numbers at one yard could be offset by posting them to another that was short of members of that particular trade. Workers could also request a transfer to another dockyard that had a vacancy in their trade and their service time would be transferred with them. Such vacancies were sometimes the sole means of gaining a promotion.

Alfred Berry transferred to Devonport because of the urgent need for many more workers as the city's Royal Dockyard, as it was grandly named, entered its final expansion stage with the building of the huge North Yard Extension. The opportunities this offered seemed obvious to a keen young man who, at the age of 25, already had 10 years' trade experience under his belt – and had a family to support with a second child on the way.

Devonport's grand project covered 114 acres, 35 of them on reclaimed land above the high water mark and the remaining 79 using the existing foreshore. It cost the country some £6 million. The focal point of the extension was a large tidal basin, 1550 feet long, 1000 feet wide and 55 feet deep. The plans also provided for three graving docks and a large entrance lock. When completed, the Royal Dockyard would have ten docks and five basins.

Alfred was there in the throng on Saturday January 13, 1905, when Lady Jackson, with some assistance from her husband, the extension's designer and builder, Sir John Jackson, opened the sluice that started the water flowing to flood the tidal basin. He was there again two years later, on Wednesday February 20, 1907, when His Royal Highness the Prince of Wales, later King George V, officially opened the North Yard Extension. This was merely a formal occasion as the basin had received its first ship, *HMS Hibernia,* six months earlier, on Friday August 10, 1906, and was already providing work for 3400 men.

In between these two soul-stirring occasions, redolent with patriotic pride, this close-knit community endured one of its most tragic and fateful events with the sinking on June 8 1905 of the submarine *A8* just off the Plymouth breakwater.

Albert and his workmates watched on that Thursday morning as the vessel moved slowly down the Sound in company with its sister ship, the

A7. They were headed for exercises in the waters off Looe, escorted by torpedo boats and Royal Navy observer craft. The *A8* made the first dive of the day just off the breakwater but as it came to the surface crew on board one of the torpedo boats noticed it had developed a list and was sitting lower and lower in the water.

Before anything could be done the *A8* slid once more below the water, but this time bow first and with her stern pointing to the sky. Within minutes she had vanished, a faulty hatch seal letting in tonnes of water that rapidly filled the submarine and, in the quaint words of one report, made it "negatively buoyant". All trim was lost and the end was inevitable. As *A8* sank, sea water at a higher pressure than the air in the boat would have forced the hatch to close tight.

As she sank to the bottom, the lives of 14 seamen and one officer were snuffed out. A few lucky ones, mostly those on the conning tower, escaped. For the rest, it was like being in a floating coffin whose lid had slammed shut. These early boats were petrol fuelled and accounts of the time report there was what appeared to be an underwater explosion.

The *A8* was raised the following Monday and transported to Devonport dockyard where the dead were removed with great dignity and respect. Albert Berry and his family were among the vast gathering of the three towns – Plymouth plus Devonport plus Stonehouse – that turned out to pay their respects the following Thursday as the funeral procession wound its way from the Devonport naval base to the cemetery.

Sailors pulled gun carriages carrying the flag draped coffins, topped by anchors made of flowers. They marched with rifles down as a military band played. At the graveside a military funeral with full honours paid respect to the tragic submariners.

....

For Albert and many of his workmates, getting to work was little more than a stroll down the hill in response to the blare of the dockyard "hooter". The yard's South Gate (also known as the Albert Road Gate) was at the foot of Albert Road in Morice Town.

Based on a design by William Scamp of the Admiralty Department of Works, this imposing structure had two towers. One contained a clock and the other housed the "hooter". A North Gate had been added in 1869 but was replaced by the St Levan Gate in 1900, which was closed in September 1966.

Street after street in nearby Morice Town was home to dockyard employees and naval staff; it was a community almost entirely dependent on seafarers and warfare. The majority of those who lived here were renters, not home-owners, and most of the imposing two-storey houses in Balfour Terrace were occupied by at least two families.

The Berrys did well. Their home at number 11 was not only brand new but was designed by one of the country's leading architectural partnerships. In 1899, local developer and builder Henry Pile had secured the approval of the Devonport council to build eight seven-room houses on a site leased from the estate of Lord St Levan of St Michael's Mount.

Not surprisingly, Mr Pile entrusted the design of the entire terrace to London-based St Aubyn and Wadling, the firm started by Lord St Levan's cousin, the Victorian architect James Piers St Aubyn (1815-1895). JP, as he was known, was renowned for his church architecture and famously missed out on getting the contract to design Truro Cathedral by one vote. His most praised work was the restoration of his cousin's home at St Michael's Mount.

Once the houses were built in the early 1900s, Mr Pile on-sold them to people such as Henry Penfound, a chief boatswain with the Royal Navy, who became Alfred and Emma's landlord soon after taking possession of number 11 on 4 May, 1904.

Two months earlier Penfound had been paid off after completing a tour of duty as a naval lieutenant on board the battleship *Repulse*, which was now resting in the dockyard at Chatham awaiting a major refit.

The Penfounds lived close by in Haddington Road – the extension of

Balfour Terrace – but Henry was often away at sea and, as one census put it, "in ports abroad". His latest tour had seen him leave home in April 1902 when the *Repulse* joined the Mediterranean Fleet for autumn exercises off Greece and Turkey with the Channel Fleet and the Cruiser Squadron. The *Repulse* didn't arrive back in Plymouth until 10 December 1903, just in time for Henry to get his affairs in order ready to become a property owner and landlord.

Alfred and Emma, with young Sydney clasping her hand, could hardly believe their luck when Henry Penfound showed them over what they hoped would be their new home. Not only was the imposing and solid house brand new but it was far more spacious than anywhere they had lived before and also had the luxury of an indoor toilet and bathroom.

'I'm letting the top floor and me and the wife will be moving in downstairs,' explained Mr Penfound. 'It's the same all along the terrace – one house, two families. We can't be having one family rattling around in a big house like this. It's still a working class area.'

Alfred and Emma had no argument with that. Their place back in Kent at 84 Saxton Street, Gillingham, although it also had an upstairs and a downstairs, seemed so much lower and smaller, and had only a single window on each floor looking out on to the street. Henry Penfound's house had big upper and lower bay windows and another window upstairs above the front door.

There was so much space – and there was a small garden out the front and another large one at the rear; no walking out of the front door and straight on to the footpath like they were used to in Saxton Street.

Emma gave Alfred's arm a squeeze and smiled up at him. She could hardly contain her delight but it wouldn't do to look too enthusiastic in front of their landlord.

'It's all very nice, Mr Penfound,' she said demurely. 'I'm sure we'll be very happy here. We'll take good care of it for you.'

And so they did for the next five years or so with Alfred applying himself to learning the many new skills demanded of the navy's shipwrights and Emma diligently ensuring they were well fed and comfortable in this brand new home which, on 29 April, 1908, saw the arrival of Wilfred Berkeley, a brother for Sydney and the man who would eventually become my father.

This Devonian link proved, however, to be but a very small twig on my family tree. Within a year, the Berrys were on the move again. Devonport's dockyard had completed its expansion and, as Britain began to hear the faint and distant rumble of the eloquently mis-named "war to end all wars", HM Dockyard's bosses decided Alfred's skills were once again required in Chatham.

And much as she had enjoyed living in Balfour Terrace, Emma was quite happy to trundle all the way back upcountry with their two young boys. They would again be among family and friends – even living for a while in Saxton Street, but this time a few doors down from their previous home and on the opposite side of the street at number 105.

For Wilfred Berkeley Berry, however, it was but the first journey in a peripatetic life that would see him maintaining his forefathers' tradition of criss-crossing the country on routes set by whatever their jobs and careers demanded. And mum, sister Judy and myself went with him.

Eventually they put down firm roots in Cornwall, but I kept moving on, not knowing whence I had come or where I belonged and only slowing down somewhat in recent years, although even now my foot is still not firmly on the brake.

WORKHOUSE WOES

WHEN Mary Anne Berry stood before the Haverfordwest Poor Law Union's receiving officer, Mr Joseph John, on Monday, July 25 1890, her life had reached its lowest ebb. As she explained to Mr John, she and her six children, who stood meekly at her side, were destitute.

'We have nothing, sir,' she said. 'I cannot feed them. No one will take us in.'

Joseph John considered the forlorn faces before him – four boys and two girls, the oldest a scrawny lad of twelve and the youngest a babe in arms, newly born and still at her mother's breast. He noted the desperation on the woman's face and the way the children gathered close to her. Their clothes were ragged and old yet there was about them a neatness and an attempt at cleanliness. He also detected pride and determination beneath the despair; this was a mother who cared.

However, he had his duty to perform; there were questions that had to be asked before incurring costs to the parish.

'And where is Mr Berry, your husband?'

'I wish I knew, sir,' whispered Mary in her broad Cockney accent, wondering how she had ever fallen for the bright young Welshman who had breezed into her life twenty years ago and whisked her away from family and friends.

'He can't earn enough to support us,' she added.

The hopes and promises of their early days together in Shoreditch had soon faded as he moved from job to job, and from town to town, while keeping her in an almost permanent state of pregnancy with seven kids in 14 years and their first-born dying when only five years old.

As the youngest brother of my great-grandfather, Alfred Jabez Berry, George Weymouth Berry had started out all right in a solid Welsh working class home. He did as his brothers and father had done before him and learned the trade of joiner and shipwright. It was an essential and worthwhile skill in a dockyard town, especially as workers could be moved between Admiralty ports if work was slack in one yard and tradesmen were needed in another.

But while older brother Alfred progressed steadily through life with gainful employment, marriage to a local girl and eventual recognition as a pillar of the local community, George had other ideas. He decided the grass was greener, and more lucrative, far from solid family life in the Berrys' house in Marine Gardens, Milford, with its view out over the Haven and the expanding dockyard on the facing shore at Pembroke. After all, as his father and brothers kept hammering into him, a man with a trade would never be short of work. Even though iron and steel were replacing timber in the nation's shipyards, carpenters would always be in demand. A man who could shape a piece of wood was sure to find gainful employment, even if it meant forsaking life close to the water. It was a trade that could be applied almost anywhere and especially in the big cities upcountry where, George reasoned, better money was surely to be made than he would ever earn in Pembroke Dock.

And so he headed for London, the River Thames and the shipyards around Woolwich and Greenwich. He reckoned there would be no problems with finding temporary lodgings as his elder brother, Joseph, now lived here in Queen Street with wife Sophie after bucking the family tradition and opting for life as a grocer.

It was here that George's path crossed that of Mary Anne Green, a true Cockney and a domestic servant in the home of John Hart, a baker running a booming business in the bustling heart of Hackney at 167

Hoxton Street. While George made good-hearted fun of Mary's Cockney whine, she quickly fell for his lilting Welsh brogue and devil-may-care ways.

When George found work harder to come by than he had ever dreamed would be the case, Mary yielded to his plea to return with him to Wales, where he believed his family's contacts would surely help him find a job and – this was the icing on the cake for Mary – they could get married.

As she stood defeated and patiently waited for Mr John to decide her fate, Mary thought ruefully back to that day on March 17, 1875 when she and George said their vows in Steynton Parish Church in front of the vicar, the Rev M B Thomas. But there was little point in dwelling on the past. Regrets were futile; what was done was done. There was no turning back of the clock. She simply knew marrying my great-uncle George had been the biggest mistake of her young life. From then on, everything went downhill.

George's hopes of work in Pembroke Dock came to nothing. So he decided they should move all the way back across the country to the Admiralty dockyard at Chatham, in Kent, which at least was closer to Mary's old home in London's East End. They obtained lodgings at 8 Woodland Terrace, Gillingham – coincidentally a short walk from where my grandfather and George's nephew, Alfred Berkeley Berry, would settle half a century later – in time for Mary to give birth on September 18, 1876 to a daughter they grandly named Adelaide Lavinia. Within months Mary was pregnant again and in July 1878 the couple welcomed their first son, John Edwin.

From then on Mary felt her life was spinning out of control. In his endless pursuit of work, George dictated a move back to Milford.

'But why, George, why?' pleaded Mary, now pregnant yet again, with second son William James who was born in July 1880.

'It's the job,' replied George. 'We go where the Admiralty tells us to. There's nothing I can do about it.'

Mary suspected there was more to it than that. She knew it was disloyal to think so but she sometimes wondered if the fault lay more with George than with the Admiralty. Other men seemed to settle into the yard's workforce and not be continually uprooting their family in the search for jobs. His own father and brothers were solid proof of that.

She had scarcely recovered from giving birth to William than they were packing up their meagre belongings yet again. George, ever optimistic, assured her it was all for the best; a good move.

'Where to this time?' asked a weary Mary.

'Portsea Island,' was George's gruff reply.

Mary had never heard of it and pressed him for more information.

'It's the place to be,' he tried to assure her. 'It's on the south coast in Hampshire, Britain's biggest island, right on the shores of the Solent and the English Channel. Plenty of good sea air for you and the kids.'

Almost as an aside he added that it was at the heart of the massive naval base at Portsmouth, one-time home of Nelson's fleet that fought the Spanish Armada and where the admiral's flagship, the *Victory*, now rested. It was in the dockyard here that he expected to find work.

One thing George certainly didn't mention was that although the booming city was blessed in part by streetlights, piped water and mains sewers, much of Portsea's housing was squalid and badly built with damp dilapidated cellars. Despite a burgeoning middle class in its outer suburbs, this was still a rough and ready naval town where crime was a regular part of daily life and the under-policed streets were rife with drunks, prostitutes, pickpockets, vagrants and beggars.

Nor did he mention, nor probably even knew, that the local death rate of children under five was well above the national average, caused by malnutrition and lack of clothing.

It was a statistic that might have caused Mary to have second thoughts. Within a year of settling into 6 Unicorn Street, Portsea, in the dirtiest, most overcrowded part of town, the eldest of her growing brood, Adelaide

Lavinia, was dead at the age of five from a combination of measles and bronchitis – and Mary was pregnant yet again.

Within months of Adelaide's death on March 20, 1882, she gave birth, in 1883, to Lillian Elizabeth and became ever more fearful for the welfare of herself and her family in Unicorn Street's squalid surroundings. Outbreaks of cholera and other epidemics were frequent and the house was damp and cold. She pleaded frequently with George for them to return to Milford where the air was cleaner and there was little of Portsea's slum-like overcrowding.

'It's not so much for me, but at least think of the children,' she urged.

Her pleading failed to move him; he seemed deaf to her demands. He had become stubborn and morose. Too often he came home with the heavy smell of beer on his breath and scant money left from his wages to pay for their food. It was as if the responsibilities of being a wage-earner and father were all too much. Yet that didn't stop him demanding his conjugal rights and once again Mary found herself pregnant. It was the final straw.

'I'm not going to bury another child here,' she snapped at him. 'You'll take us back to Milford or me and the kids will make our own way there.'

Living conditions in Robert Street, Milford's busy commercial hub one block back from the cliff-top harbourfront, was little better. Mary, with five children under 10 and a husband who lacked the drive and commitment she noted in the rest of the Berry clan, was burdened with drudgery and worry. She was grateful for what money George so grudgingly gave and reluctantly tolerated his surly insistent presence to the extent that even though it had become a loveless marriage she again found herself pregnant within a year of Ada's birth.

This was the final straw. Less than six months after delivering Albert Edward from her womb, Mary threw herself and her children on the mercy of the guardians of the grim Haverfordwest Poor Law Union workhouse.

As she watched Joseph John's pen inscribe her details on to the forms in front of him she thought again about her response. Did she really wish she knew where George had gone; did she even care? All she was concerned about was caring for her family and George could take care of himself.

'I don't really know where he is, sir,' she said. 'He's gone, and left us with nothing. Last I heard he was boarding with a widow lady up by Robert Street, in Manchester Square.'

The receiving officer's face remained impassive. Every day he heard stories of neglect, desertion, sickness and abject poverty and of families who could not put food on the table, fuel on the fire or shoes on their children's feet. He could not afford to display emotion or appear to favour one unfortunate over another, even though he knew some were more deserving than others; that there were those who made no attempt to improve themselves and others to whom the workhouse was a refuge of last resort and were almost too proud to depend on its charity.

Mr John sensed the woman standing before him was firmly in the latter category. She had been reduced to shedding the remnants of her pride and was here out of desperation for the welfare of her children. He signed the forms with a flourish.

'You will be admitted and placed in the care of Mr Thomas,' he said. 'You will be a charge against the parish and your first meals will be supper.'

Mary took a long deep breath of relief. Her shoulders drooped as the tension ebbed. This was not where she wanted to be but it meant the children would be fed and have a roof over their heads.

'Thank you, sir,' she said. 'I am truly grateful.'

Mary and the children filed slowly through the entrance door into the main workhouse block to be met by the institution's master, John Thomas, and the matron, Martha Martin. Mr Thomas, a sombre-looking 51-year-old, had somewhat unusually been allowed to continue as master despite the recent death of his wife, Annie, who had previously served as the workhouse matron.

Rather than follow the usual procedure and seek a married couple following Annie Thomas's death, the guardians had appointed Martha

Martin, the 30-year-old daughter of the assistant overseer at the nearby St Thomas Green Infirmary to take her place, although John Thomas continued to hope that his eldest daughter, Maud, would eventually return from her training as a nurse at the vast and highly praised Crumpsall workhouse in Manchester with its infirmary and specialist wards and room for 1600 inmates.

John Thomas nodded a greeting at Mary and conducted a hurried roll call, checking her name and those of the children against a large register spread out on a table in front of him. He folded the book shut, his duties done.

'I'll leave you with matron,' he said. 'Wait here and the doctor will be with you soon.'

There would be no admission into the grim rooms beyond until they had undergone the inevitable medical examination for lice, vermin and signs of disease or open sores. The children's hair was cropped right back. Then came the humiliating experience of being stripped, bathed and issued with a workhouse uniform. Their clothes were taken away to be washed, disinfected and stored until they were ready to return to the outside world. Finally came the worst moment of all – the heart wrenching separation as the children were removed from Mary's close attention and the boys were divided from the girls.

Mary held on tight to baby Albert and kept her face averted to hide her tears as she wrapped her free arm in a tight hug around each of the other children in turn.

'We'll be together soon,' she whispered in a brave attempt at reassurance as a young female assistant summoned by the matron led them off to their separate wards in different blocks of the workhouse.

It was an optimistic but forlorn promise. For the next four years, Mary and her children spent much of their lives in the small, dirty, poorly ventilated and badly heated wards enclosed by the thick stone walls of this gaunt institution. On several occasions she obtained permission to leave but inevitably she returned, sometimes merely for an overnight stay – in before supper and out after breakfast – and on other occasions to spend time with her children. Always her conduct was recorded as 'good' and her prime concern was the welfare of her children.

Years of deprivation, sub-standard housing and poor nutrition had, however, taken their toll. Much more so than was indicated by the single annotation that she was 'unwell' when she asked to be taken in for an overnight stay on Thursday August 20 1891. With year-old Albert in her arms she sought a bed and a meal. She stayed for supper – a greasy wooden bowl of weak gruel – and breakfast, which was much the same but with the addition of a chunk of bread.

She struggled on and began the new year by securing 12-year-old son John's discharge so that he could stay with his uncle in London. But her own health was getting no better in the cold Welsh winter and on Saturday April 23, 1892, she was discharged by the workhouse to go into the Haverfordwest Infirmary for an unspecified operation. Several weeks later, on Thursday June 22, she and son John reappeared before receiving officer Joseph John seeking readmission to the workhouse. John had been sent back from his uncle in London as "unwell" and Mary was returning from the infirmary.

And so she battled on, seeking escape from the confines of the workhouse yet drawn back time and again to spend even a few moments with her children. Always her conduct was 'good' and she seemed to come and go almost at will despite the seemingly rigid conditions laid down by the Poor Law Act and by the local guardians.

Through it all there was never a mention or a record of husband George. As Mary had informed the workhouse receiving officer, on the night of the 1891 census George was listed as a shipwright boarding in the house of widow Albina Phillips and her son in Manchester Square, Steynton – now Milford Haven. After that he disappeared completely from official view until, on January 8, 1897, at the age of 43, Mary gave birth to Florence

Sophia and George's name appeared on the birth certificate as the girl's father.

On Thursday August 9, 1892, Mary asked to be readmitted to the workhouse. Her reason was basic and enough to touch the hardest heart.

'I can't bear to be parted from my sons,' she told the receiving officer.

She was given dinner and supper and left the next day after breakfast, taking sons John, now a hardened lad of 14, and William, 12, with her.

Sadly, no matter how much Mary tried, life on the outside could not be sustained and the family continued to rely on the workhouse for their food and lodgings. Her frail and sick body didn't help and she was sent from the workhouse to the infirmary on Tuesday May 2, 1893, for an operation on her face. A week later she was back with her children in the workhouse.

They remained there throughout the summer, although Mary would make occasional forays out into the town, keeping in touch with her few friends and alert for any news of her wayward husband. It was a sporadic and low-key version of what today would be labelled as networking – a finger on the weak pulse of opportunities, a street-wise eye open for any avenue of survival.

It meant she was again able to offer a special reason when pleading for a discharge from the workhouse on Monday October 2. There was a gleam of pride in her eyes as she put her case.

'I want to take my son John,' she explained. 'He has work. I am putting him to service as an errand boy.'

For John it meant the end of more than three years of sleeping on a chaff mattress laid on three wooden planks on an iron bedstead; of subsisting on monotonous meals of gruels, stews and bread; of being confined for exercise and fresh air to the courtyards between the accommodation blocks; of being cold in winter and almost suffocated in summer. Whatever employment, whatever master he was going to, would be better than this.

Soon, however, he decided a precarious existence pedalling around the streets of Haverfordwest as an errand boy was not for him. He enlisted in the Royal Navy as a boy second class and went on to serve right through the Great War until being demobbed on November 18, 1919, having risen only as far as the lowly rank of able-bodied seaman. He was sent on his way with the Naval Medal, the Victory Star, a war gratuity and a naval pension.

John may have been off her hands, but Mary still had five other children in the workhouse to fret over. Their welfare was also her prime concern and on Saturday November 4 1893, she asked permission to take 11-year-old Lillian away to Milford for a week.

'It's for the good of her health,' Mary told the officer considering her application. 'A bit of sea air and she has cousins there.'

She made no mention of the fact that it was also in Milford – in Manchester Square halfway along Robert Street where the cousins lived – that husband George had last been living.

The request was granted, as workhouse manager John Thomas duly noted in the register of admissions and discharges. Almost a month later, on Thursday, November 30, he recorded Lillian's return and that she was to receive the special Class 7 children's diet. This tended to have a bit more meat and perhaps some milk or tea in addition to the staples of vegetable broth and bread served to the adults in greater measure, although it was hardly a sufficient barrier to the bone-chilling Welsh winter.

Branded as paupers and sustained by the workhouse, the family struggled on through Christmas and the new year. The one absentee, William, who had been on the outside for almost eighteen months, working in the grocery shop of his cousin Dundas Berry in Woolwich, was – in the terse words of Mr Thomas's register – "returned to his mother" on February 22, 1894. London was not for him: the 14-year-old was destitute and hungry. The workhouse had become the only "home" he knew.

Mary, however, remained undaunted. She was determined there would be a better life for her children. On May 30 she was allowed to take Ada out of the workhouse "to go to Mr Lewis" where the 10-year-old set out on the trail taken by so many working class girls, her mother included, and went "into service" as a domestic servant.

Mary returned to the workhouse with Lillian and Albert on Monday August 27. They had dinner and supper and left after breakfast the next day – the last time there is any record of them in the Haverfordwest Poor Law Union's workhouse register.

When she surprisingly gave birth on January 8, 1897, to Florence Sophia she was living in Grove Row, Haverfordwest, a laneway close to the Oak Inn on St Thomas Green. On the registration of the birth she put husband George, shipwright journeyman, as the father. This raises more questions than it answers. Where had he been all the time his wife and kids were living in the workhouse? Why was he living in relative comfort as a boarder while they were confined within the grim walls of an institution? The most charitable answer is that although he could not earn enough to pay for rent and food for the entire family, he could scrape by as a "single" man. As a journeyman (one who is paid by the day, or a casual in present terminology) he would have good days and bad days and sometimes have a run of employment enough to feed himself and Mary and maybe one or more of the children – which would explain her random comings and goings at the workhouse.

By the time of the 1901 census Mary's workhouse days and life as a pauper appeared to be behind her. She was again living in St Thomas Green, listed as married but with no sign of husband George. Four of her children – Ada, Albert, Joseph and Florence – were still with her. William was working for his grocer uncle, Dundas Berry, in Samuel Street, Woolwich; John was an able seaman in the Royal Navy and there is no record of what Lily was doing at that time.

By 1911 Ada had met and married, on August 22, John James from Haverfordwest, a signalman with the Great Western Railway. She died in Haverfordwest in 1963 at the age of 78. Lily reappeared in 1912 when she apparently married William James, quite possibly the brother of Ada's husband, in Haverfordwest.

Joseph, who found work as a boot and shoe salesman, hardly reached adulthood. He died from a dilated heart in the Haverfordwest infirmary on April 30, 1908, at the age of 20. Mary, her body frail from years of childbirth, malnutrition, impoverishment and endless stress, died from heart disease on February 16, 1910, with son William at her side. But at least she had the consolation of knowing none of her surviving children nor any of their offspring were likely to again be labelled as impoverished and destitute paupers.

John was pensioned out of the navy after seeing World War 1 service on HMS *Berwick* and eventually died of phthisis or tuberculosis of the lungs in Pontardwe, Glamorgan, in November 1934.

What became of the elusive George remains a mystery still being worked on. He was not present at the death of either wife Mary or their son Joseph and when Ada married John James he was recorded as deceased. He may have gone to sea, as many shipwrights did, or even sought a new life overseas.

But there are no records to support such theories and the fact that Ada knew of his death suggests he remained in the Milford area and kept well away from his family as well as staying well clear of any form of officialdom – even to the extent of leaving no record of his death.

Several other researchers have helped in my bid to track him down. It has been suggested he emigrated or went to sea, where he could use his skills as a ship's carpenter. But he appears on no shipping records, passenger lists or immigration files.

There are no clues as to how or why he was given the unusual second name of Weymouth. Maybe he was conceived in the resort of the same name during a holiday excursion by his parents, William and Ann. It gives him the defining sort of tag that is usually so useful when trawling through lists and records and trying to separate one George from another. Yet the only other George Weymouth Berry so far found in numerous global searches was married in Sydney in 1912 and proved to have no connection whatsoever with my Milford Haven George.

And so he remains my mysterious disappearing grand-uncle until some fellow researcher produces some additional clues.

FARM HANDS AND SERVANT GIRLS

AN OLD LANE LEADING NOWHERE

FAMILY historians can find themselves going to places which, once they are there, are revealed as sad destinations few would ever want to visit. Hollington is one such place.

A couple of centuries ago this dot on the map was a small agricultural village. It was built amid the gentle Sussex hills on land trampled upon by King William's hordes as his Norman conquerors made their way to London. My ancestors have lived there, as farm labourers and paupers, since at least the early 1600s.

Today, it is a dreary suburban no man's land. Blocks of public housing stand where the cottages of my forebears once looked out over fertile fields. Few recognisable landmarks remain. It has been described by local historians as 'the lost village'. They don't mince words but say Hollington was 'gutted' by redevelopment and wholesale land clearances in the 1960s. Nearly three hundred properties were demolished to transform this former rural community into what is now a downmarket suburb of nearby Hastings.

We stand by a low brick wall where Hollington Old Lane joins the main Hastings to Battle road. The wall separates the footpath from a scrubby garden alongside the Tivoli Tavern, built in the 1860s and most likely where the men of my Britt clan, the maternal side of the family, drank their beer at the end of a long day in the fields. True to form, it is the pubs that remain when all else vanishes and the Tivoli is one of a clutch of hostelries that provide the only remnants of Hollington's past.

From the pub, Hollington Old Lane descends on much the same route it took in great-great-grandfather's day, curving gently down to the valley floor and winding up the other side to link up with Old Church Road. The terraces of cottages have been replaced by a mish-mash of dwellings from diverse eras and in clashing styles – from late Victorian stolid through '60s utilitarian to modern garish; very little of it in tune with its surroundings and all dominated by three high-rise towers of public housing.

We walked its length, an old map and a street directory from 1900 as our guide. But to no avail. Not a smidgen of William Britt's home or surroundings remained. Havelock Terrace and Havelock Cottages were no more. Gone, too, were the cycle works, the laundry, the two schools – one for boys, one for girls – the blacksmith, the general store and the waterworks with its engine house. All obliterated. And the fields which my family's cottages once overlooked – and provided them with work – are buried under a conglomeration of buildings that proves neither public nor private developers are immune to creating ugliness.

Hollington was never a thriving or prosperous place. For most of its existence since way back in the 14th century its population hardly exceeded three hundred and few of these were landowners. The occupation of many whose names appear on the parish registers is stated bluntly as 'pauper', as if poverty was a lifetime's vocation. It was what today's cliché-ridden media would describe as a close-knit community; living, working, marrying and dying within the narrow confines of a small rural parish.

The nearest thing to prosperity occurred when the Battle Road and the Hollington-Hastings turnpike were built in the mid-1800s. These links brought hitherto unseen traffic as dairy farms and market gardens grew up to supply nearby urban areas and the population soared to 1053 at the time of the 1871 census.

At the start of World War II – which saw the entire area under constant attack with Hollington Old Lane right in the thick of it – there were 7500 people living there. Today, it is nothing more than a dreary suburb gobbled up by Hastings' inland spread.

Fortunately, the Britts, the Gates and the Ashdowns decided not to hang around. They found fresher, more productive fields elsewhere, some as far away as New Zealand, and moved outward, onward and upward. Hollington is now but another sad way station on my family's ascent from labouring, poverty and the workhouse.

Their names remain penned against baptisms, marriages and deaths in the famed Church in the Wood, rebuilt in 1865 on a site some authorities say shows Saxon remains while others settle for claiming the traces as Norman. But my ancestors and their kinfolk wisely forsook these ancient roots and have long moved on, once again leaving next to nothing for the family historian to explore or treasure.

And so we take our pictures of these neglected remnants of our rural past and fall back on our imagination to recreate the lives and times of these tillers and toilers of the Sussex Downs.

AN INDUSTRIOUS TIME AT SCHOOL

WHEN Catherine Gates, began spitting up blood and shivering with an acute fever the writing was well and truly on the wall. Husband George knew the signs. The winter of 1869 had already taken its toll on many of Brighton's poorer (and not so poor) residents as they succumbed to the damp and cold. But what had hit Catherine, my great-great-grandmother, was no ordinary seasonal chill.

As George drove on his rounds as a delivery man for beer retailer William Kemble, he had heard all the talk on the streets of the many people falling prey to a virulent and wasting disease. It was then known as phthisis or consumption and the word was out that there was no known cure. Only much later did it became more simply labelled as TB – the dreaded tuberculosis for which no antibiotic was discovered until 1943. As he listened to Catherine's hacking cough and tried to swab away her sweat, George had no doubt about the grim future awaiting them. Never a robust woman, Catherine was already visibly thinner and frailer than a few days ago. The disease was eating away at her insides, attacking her lungs, infecting other organs. She was wasting away as he and their nine children, six of them under 12, looked on in their crowded, airless terrace home at 5 Circus Grove.

Fresh air and sunshine were the only prescriptions that doctors could offer anyone battling what had become one of the greatest killers of the nineteenth century. And they were rare treats that the working classes could only dream about. There would be no curative escape to the rarefied retreats of Swiss sanitoria for the likes of Catherine.

George looked at his wife's emaciated body and knew there was little hope. His body language spoke volumes to the children. They huddled together, well aware what the future would bring.

Events took their inevitable and painful course and Catherine eventually gave up her struggle for life on March 26, 1870. Equally inevitable was the fate awaiting George and the younger children. With no mother to care for a two-year-old boy and five girls under 12, George knew the workhouse was the only way he could guarantee they had a roof over their heads, a bed to sleep on and three meals a day, however basic those meals might be.

'It's for the best,' he told the girls as they waited to be paraded before the Poor Law guardians. 'It won't be for ever and we'll still be together.'

He was only partly right. Being committed to the workhouse was certainly better than being cast out on to the streets to fend for themselves. But the system was such that George and two-year-old James were classified as paupers and allotted accommodation at the reasonably new Elm Grove workhouse on Race Hill Road while Agnes, Martha, Clara, Mary and Harriet became 'inmates' at the Warren Farm Industrial School. There was to be no family togetherness.

'Home' for George and James was now a solid and imposing building completed only three years before their arrival. The impressive T-shaped main block rose four storeys beneath a central clock tower. Iron gates in the corridors separated the male inmates from the females. A wing at the centre of the main block included a large chapel and further away was a 'lunatics' block, an infirmary and short-term and fever wards.

Many of the 700 inmates – all classified as paupers - had been transferred there from the old Church Hill workhouse. That institution had been quickly demolished and the site sold for prestige housing – giving a handy overall profit for the guardians of £1000, even after allowing for the cost of an innovative system of artificial ventilation at Elm Grove.

'At least the air here is fit to breathe,' said one bent and frail old man to George as he held James in his arms and waited to be checked by the officers and nurse and be shown where they were to sleep.

'It's not easy with the young ones, is it?' said a sympathetic voice alongside. 'Specially not for a man.' She flicked a finger in James's direction. 'Seems we've got two of a kind.'

The woman was slight and thin and had the ends of her long shawl wrapped around a boy about James's size and age who stood at her side, clutching her hand.

'Mine's just turned two,' she said. 'What's yours?' ... with a nod of her head at James.

'Same,' said George. 'His mum died a few weeks back.'

'And mine doesn't have a dad,' said the woman, with a flick of her eyes towards her own boy. 'There's another lad but he's older and they won't take him here. He's with his gran over in Jubilee Street. Almost next door to Mr Giles, the town crier. She owns her own house but it seems there's no room for us.' She gave a defiant shrug of her shoulders. 'Anyhow, I wanted the little one to be with me.'

George offered a weak smile back. He wondered if there was more to the story than she was telling. He felt he should say something more, offer some information about himself in response to the woman's outpourings.

'My missus would've done the same,' he said. 'Wanted the young ones with her. Especially the girls.'

The woman stretched out a consoling hand and rested it briefly on his forearm.

'Oh, you poor thing. Girls too. Boys can take care of themselves but girls ...' Her voice tapered off, her opinion clear but unspoken.

'There was another lad, David, but he was only with us for a few months,' said George in a flat unemotional voice that accepted infant deaths as the norm rather than the exceptional.

They continued talking as they waited their turn to endure the demeaning and intrusive admission process. She gave her name as Elizabeth Allcorn and her son's as George. He was finding her easy to talk to and confided that he hoped to leave the workhouse whenever he could and continue working as a fly driver.

'It all depends on what will happen to the lad while I'm away,' he said. 'If I can get summat regular we won't have to stay here too long. And there's the girls, too; I worry what's happening to them.'

There was a lull in their conversation, each numbed by their surroundings and their situation, inward looking and contemplating what lay ahead. George was aware of the woman taking occasional sideways glances in his direction. Again she reached out and touched him gently on the arm.

'Perhaps they'd let me look after your lad while you're out working,' she said. 'Make it easier for you.'

She gave an encouraging smile. George hesitated; took a while to react. The stranger's words eventually sunk in and he smiled back. He let out a deep breath: relief at a burden being eased, at hearing an offer of help and kindness when he had never felt so low. It was an arrangement he readily accepted and one for which workhouse governor Edward Sattin gave his approval. It would be one less infant for Emma, his wife and workhouse matron, to worry about and would ensure the child's father was free to search for work and eventually have no more need for their support. And the woman apparently was a skilled needle-worker so would be able to earn her keep helping the housekeeping staff.

Although James remained in the women's quarters with Elizabeth, they were able to meet up with George briefly at meal times and occasionally they took a stroll in the small garden space between the workhouse and the infirmary. Such meetings were encouraged by governor Sattin and his wife, who themselves had six children aged from four to 13 living on the premises.

Promoted from workhouse clerk and assistant matron, the Sattins had brought a caring benevolence to an institution that in recent years had gained local notoriety under four previous governors described in the *Brighton Herald* as two insolvent tradesmen and two unsuccessful schoolmasters, one of whom had absconded even after having his salary raised from £80 to £90 a year. The couple's tenure was later recognised by the erection of a plaque acknowledging Mr Sattin's 32 years' service as workhouse governor.

With James providing a strong link between them, George and Elizabeth gradually grew closer. They looked forward to their meetings and became more relaxed in each other's company.

'It's good having you here and helping out with the young fellow,' he told her over an evening meal of mutton suet pudding and the daily pint of beer.

'He's no trouble and it means my George has got a playmate,' she assured him. 'They get on well together.'

'Like us, eh?'

She smiled and put a hand on his.

'Yes, George. Like us.'

Having Elizabeth taking care of James meant George felt relaxed about getting away from the workhouse and taking whatever driving jobs were going. He had no intention of being labelled a pauper for any longer than necessary. Soon, he hoped, he would be assured of regular work, at least enough to support himself and James. And there were times when he slipped into a bit of a daydream while slowly threading his horse and cart through Brighton's crowded and narrow lanes and wondered if one day Elizabeth might be sharing her time with him outside, rather than within, the confines of the workhouse. There were also his daughters to think about, especially the youngest, Harriett, who was only five years old. He could only hope that the older girls – Agnes, 8, Martha, 9, Mary, 10, and Clara, 13, my great-grandmother – would be able to take care of her.

George knew full well by talking to others who had seen their children sent to Warren Farm that it was a harsh and unforgiving place. Conditions and discipline were beyond strict; they were brutal. Children even as young as Harriett would have to break the ice on water piped up from what was then the deepest dug well in the world in order to have a wash. For even minor misdemeanours they could be made to sit in a bath of freezing water. Beatings with a hairbrush were frequent.

The only solace for George was that Warren Farm was intended to be a school as well as a poorhouse. The boy inmates were taught gardening, tailoring and boot making, while the girls were instructed in domestic service. There was thus every chance that when the time came for them to leave, the girls would at least have sufficient skills to enable them to obtain work. And if they could survive the harsh and callous treatment inside those high, glass-topped walls – and also escape the tuberculosis and other diseases that afflicted so many of the young inmates – they would surely be able to cope with the world outside.

'It's all for the best that they learn these things,' he confided to Elizabeth. 'Heaven knows how I'll ever be able to support them.'

She held his hand and gave it an affectionate squeeze. George was aware this physical contact had happened more and more on their brief times together. It roused feelings that had lain dormant for some time since the death of Catherine and all the upheavals that had followed. They seemed to have much in common and there was no doubt a shared warmth of feeling.

'Don't you fret about the girls,' advised Elizabeth. 'They'll be taught well to fetch and carry and cook and clean and they'll soon be off your hands and into the arms of some other man.'

George heard himself reacting to her words; his voice driven by some deep and uncontrolled impulse.

'And what about you? Will you be finding some other man?'

She shot him a sudden glance, half smile and half surprise. He saw her face redden. She let go of his hand and for a while stayed silent; looking away and seeming to retreat inside herself, her thoughts elsewhere.

'There's no one for me out there,' she said, gesturing beyond the workhouse walls.

Unbidden inner forces drove George onward, expressing thoughts he had so far kept to himself.

'And in here?'

The words hung between them. Both knew what he meant. But he rushed on, stumbling and mumbling as he voiced his hidden feelings.

'We could make a go of it. The boys are like a couple of brothers. And we're two of a kind. I've lost my missus and you ...'

'No George.' She cut in and grasped his hand firmly in hers. 'It's not like that. I'm no widow woman. My George doesn't have a dad; never did. Same with the other lad, Walter. That's why my ma's not having me staying with her. I'm a bit of a bad lot I suppose; never married.'

She gave a shrug of resignation and drew her shawl closer around her, waiting apprehensively for George's reaction. He remained silent for a while before easing his hand from her grasp and placing it gently back on tops of hers.

'I see no problem with that,' he said. 'You wouldn't be the only woman in that situation. Makes no difference to me.'

And so, in the summer of 1875, he and Elizabeth were married and set up home in Essex Place, Brighton, with their sons Walter, George and James. Another son, William, was born soon after and two years later Elizabeth gave birth to her first daughter, another Elizabeth.

True to his hopes, all George's daughters had by then emerged from Warren Farm Industrial School to find work and homes. Martha and Mary eventually plucked up the courage to sail away to the far side of the world to find work, husbands and middle-class prosperity in New Zealand. Agnes lived with her eldest sister, Catherine, and her large family in Hollington. Harriett stayed in Brighton working as a servant in Sheen's beer house in George Street, Brighton. And Clara, my great-grandmother, moved to Hollington to marry Stephen Britt.

Agnes died aged 27 and Harriett at 35 and one cannot help but wonder how much havoc was wreaked on their health by the conditions they had to endure in childhood and at the notorious Warren Farm institution.

THE MIGRANTS

ALMOST A KIWI

IF things had gone according to plan I might now be the grandfather of a brood of Kiwis rather than two young Australians. I might have also not had to wait another 40 years to discover the existence of a long-lost branch line of the family started by a brother and two sisters of my maternal grandmother.

When life went pear-shaped back in the UK in the mid 1960s, the best solution seemed to be the one I've always tended to follow when trouble looms – run away as far as possible. And what could be further away from dear old Pommieland than wild, wet and woolly New Zealand?

Nascent thoughts of a long-haul escape from endless commuting and an unsettled home life were further stimulated by buddy, workmate and best-man John Clift telling me the *New Zealand Herald* was running advertisements seeking journalist migrants. He had already replied and got a favourable response.

Where John went, I followed. We had started out as apprentice reporters on the staid and august *West Briton*, in Cornwall, in the far southwest of England where druids, magic-carpet salesmen and the ghost of King Arthur still roamed. Once my National Service stint as a petty criminal in Royal Air Force uniform ended I joined him in the reporters' room at the *Worthing Gazette*. When he later blazed the trail towards the journalists' mecca of Fleet Street, I again followed.

The offices of *Travel Trade Gazette* were actually off-Fleet Street but near enough for us to smell the ink on the dailies and rub shoulders with their by-lined stars at boozy pub lunches. Anyway, who cared? The big boys were lucky to chase a story further south than Brighton Pier whereas we travelled the globe. For the next five years John and I worked together in a dream job as travel industry reporters, roving the world in luxury and excess.

With such a history of follow my leader, sending an application and a CV to the *New Zealand Herald* was inevitable. Acceptance and rejection followed in quick succession. My skills were OK but my wife Hazel's renal problems, detected at the medical examination, were not, despite the fact she was managing to work full-time and run a home. Natural selection was alive and well in the far-off antipodes.

Likewise in Australia. After firing off letters hither and thither in a furious response to the Kiwi knock-back I landed a job with Peter Isaacson Publications in Melbourne only to encounter the same hard-line response from Australia House. That is, until the irascible yet loveable Peter Isaacson used his formidable contacts as a much-lauded wartime hero to get the decision overturned. Australia House, however, still demanded we lodge a two-thousand pound bond and surrender our passports for two years. So much for the concept of assisted migration and ten-pound tourists.

But at least we were on our way, flying via such places as Bombay, Rangoon and Darwin and eventually landing on June 8, 1966 on a cold and dreary Saturday morning at an equally dreary Essendon airport where the only refreshment was a weak Nescafe into which a surly waitress inexplicably floated a slice of lemon.

New Zealand had become a forgotten dream.

Not once in all the many years I knew her did my grandmother, Catherine Newsome (nee Britt) ever speak of New Zealand or show any sign of knowing of its existence. Nor did she even once mention that two of her aunts had made the incredible decision to leave the narrow confines of servitude in a Sussex seaside town and start new lives in the furthest corner of the world. There was never the faintest hint that the family had Kiwi cousins. Nor that her own sister, Eva, had married a preacherman and started a new life in Vermont, the heartland of Methodism in the USA. Not even my own decision to embark on a similar venture sparked a memory of these long-ago fellow migrants. They simply did not exist in memory or family mementoes.

The letter that young Martha Gates received at her sister Clara's home in the Sussex village of Hollington in the spring of 1883 has certainly long gone. A visit from the postman was a rare event at their cottage in Old Lane. An enveloped bearing a New Zealand stamp was even rarer. Little wonder therefore that several of the Gates and Britt families – her brothers and sisters, nephews and nieces – were clustered around the kitchen table when Martha arrived home weary and dirty. It was the end of another long and arduous day toiling 'below stairs' as a cook in one of the grand houses three kilometres down the road in Hastings.

It took her a while to realise she was the focus of their attention – she and a buff-coloured envelope placed prominently in the middle of the sturdy wooden table.

Brother-in-law Stephen Britt nodded towards the envelope and gently pushed it across the table in Martha's direction.

'A letter Martha. For you. The stamp says it's from New Zealand.'

She detected a tremor in his voice; stolid Stephen, a rough and ready builder's labourer, was actually a bit excited. She caught his mood and perked up. The sense of anticipation among her nieces and nephews was infectious. They all guessed it was from her brother, George, but it was what he might have to say that was making everyone nervous.

George, my great-grand-uncle, was no great letter-writer in frequency or content. His schooling had been minimal. He had run away to sea at the age of 12 to join the crew of a sailing ship carrying nitre from Chile to England. The old windjammers he worked on took him around treacherous Cape Horn on several occasions. They also made several trips to New Zealand where he eventually jumped ship and settled in Totara North, which happily promotes itself as a quaint sleepy backwater on the shores of Whangaroa Harbour and, fittingly for an old seafarer, supplied the timber for more than seventy Pacific trading boats in the late 1800s.

Martha knew George was more skilled in rope splicing than penning words and thus she treasured all the more the brief note she had received from him not long after he had settled into his new surroundings. Its terse, semi-literate message had been a constant cheering antidote to her days of drudgery in the sculleries and kitchens where she laboured six and a half days a week. Already her hopes were soaring that this latest letter was the sequel and longed-for climax to that earlier note. She fumbled with the envelope, her hopes and anxieties mingling as she pulled out the folded single sheet of thin-lined exercise book paper.

One hand went to her mouth, stifling a gasp. The other held the letter out to Stephen.

'Oh, he's done it,' she said. 'I've got to tell Mary.'

She was almost out of the door before Clara called out, 'Tell her what? What's happening Martha?'

Stephen answered for her as he laid the sheet of spidery scrawl in the table for all to read.

'They're going to New Zealand,' he said in his slow Sussex drawl. 'George is fixin' it for them to emigrate. He reckons it's a better life for the young lasses. Maybe he's right.'

There was, however, an underlying doubt and a sad resignation in his voice. He couldn't see why anyone would want to leave all their family and friends and sail away to the far side of the world. What made New Zealand any better than England anyway? He turned away from the table, making room for others to peruse the letter and spoke to Clara.

'What's for supper, mother? Better not wait for Martha; reckon she'll be gone awhile.'

Martha was well into her trek back into Hastings before she realised that amid all the fuss she had left her letter in the kitchen table. But it didn't matter; it was what George had written that was most important and what Mary would want to know. This would be their escape from a life of hardship that offered little hope of improvement. Firmly entrenched in her mind were memories of the years she, Mary and their sisters Clara, Agnes and Harriet had spent in the Brighton Industrial School after their mother had died. Despite its name, the daunting brick pile was in reality little more than a workhouse with hours of unrelenting drudgery. The institution's educational aspect was less a grounding in literacy and numeracy but concentrated more on training the female inmates in the domestic chores that were deemed to be their inevitable lot in life.

Buoyed by excitement she scurried along the road and to the grand three-storey home of the Oakley family at 21 Cornwallis Gardens. There she carefully descended the concrete steps into the basement area and tapped timidly at the brass knocker on the door used only by tradesmen and servants. She hoped it would be Mary who would answer. She was bursting with her news. The door inched cautiously open. Ann Cooper, the Oakleys' other domestic servant, stood there looking hot and flustered.

'Oh, it's you Ann,' said Martha, not failing to hide her disappointment that her sister hadn't answered the door and then realising she must have sounded terribly rude. 'I hoped I could speak to Mary. I've got some good news.'

Ann brushed a stray hair back off her brow. She wiped her hands down her apron and summoned up a tired smile.

'We're flat out cleaning the pots and the stove. The family's got guests for dinner tonight.'

She paused. Her smile broadened. Martha's mood was infectious.

'It looks like your news can't wait. You creep through to the scullery and I'll tell Mary you're here. But don't keep her too long.'

'Thanks Ann. I know how busy you are. Promise, I'll be very quick.'

She knew it was a bad time to call. Evening service was always stressful and busy, especially if the family had guests to dinner. By then most of the staff were sure to be weary and frazzled. The two girls would have been hard at work since rising dutifully from their beds at six o'clock. They had only half an hour to make their beds, get washed and dressed, with their hair tied neatly back beneath their caps, and be downstairs to stoke the kitchen range into life to boil water for the household's early morning tea.

From then on they faced a demanding day of almost non-stop physical activity with brief stops for meals and maybe a short rest break in mid-afternoon. Mary and Ann were expected to sweep, dust, polish, clean, wash, fetch and carry from early morning until quite late at night. There were heavy buckets of warm water to be carried up the stairs for bathing and weighty pots and pans to be scrubbed and scoured in the kitchen. Scuttles of coal had to be lugged from room to room to feed the fireplaces. It was dawn to dusk drudgery that earned the girls about ten pounds a year. To Martha's mind, even though she earned almost double that as a cook, there was no way they could be any worse off in New Zealand, especially as she'd heard society there was more relaxed and there were more opportunities for young women to get on. She drew her coat tighter round her and shuffled her feet on the scullery's hard bluestone floor. At least the weather would be better than the endless chilly damp of the Sussex coast.

The door swung open as a breathless Mary rushed in, drying her hands on a piece of towelling, her face flushed and sweaty but smiling broadly. Her words spilled out in her excitement.

'Oh Martha, don't tell me. Let me guess. It's George. He's going to help us get to New Zealand.'

Martha could only nod in response. Her sister's exuberance was overwhelming. They clutched at each other and hugged.

'A letter arrived today but I was in such a rush to tell you I left it behind.'

'It doesn't matter. We're going, we're going.'

They embraced again, tears of joy welling up. Their celebration was cut short by Ann calling from the kitchen for Mary to come and help. They kissed and parted, Mary rushing off back to the kitchen and Martha letting herself out on to the basement stairs and buoyed to face the walk back to Hollington.

Domestic help was such an important aspect of Victorian life that almost 13 per cent of the women of England and Wales were employed in this capacity during the 19th century. A well-managed household had anywhere between one and forty or more staff, depending upon the size of the home or estate and the needs of the family. Even the middle class scraped together enough extra money to hire at least one servant.

Engagement of staff followed a rigid hierarchy. Lowest on the pecking order, and often the first to be employed, was the "daily girl" or "charwoman" – usually a job taken by a girl in her teens who was responsible for general housekeeping and heavy cleaning.

Depending upon the number of other staff, she might have laundry and other responsibilities as well. She was a Cinderella without the help of a fairy godmother. The next to be hired would usually be either a housemaid or a nursemaid depending upon the age of the children in the home.

The housemaid would assist with serving meals and guests, "freshening" the parlour, turning down the beds and helping the lady of the house with her personal needs.

Sometimes she might provide domestic services to other house staff of higher rank.

A nurse or nursemaid would have been employed to take care of small children. If possible this post would be filled by someone from more highly educated circles of Victorian society rather than the domestic servant class.

The nursemaid provided all of the services normally provided by today's nanny. She dressed the children, bathed and fed them, took them outside to play, and acted in like a mother in many ways. Sometimes a "wet nurse" was employed to breast feed infants in Victorian homes.

The next to be hired would normally be the cook. She had absolute authority over the kitchen and, in homes where there were no domestic staff beyond the charwoman and a housemaid, was often responsible for supervising and hiring the domestic help as well.

This trio of chargirl, nurse or housemaid and cook was capable of providing a wide range of services to the smaller and less affluent Victorian families. For larger households, the hiring progression continued with the next in line usually being a male attendant. Depending upon the home, his responsibilities ranged from general maintenance to providing valet services to the lord of the mansion. He might also double as the stable keeper and drive the carriage.

For all, the hours were long and the pay was dismal, but there was a sense of pride in being a valued domestic. Many servants spent a lifetime with the same employer and often watched the children grow into the new lords and ladies of the manor. It was from the inevitability of this life that the two Gates girls decided to escape.

In the spring of 1884 Martha and Mary Gates paused on the dock at the Thames-side port of Tilbury and looked up in awe at the four slender masts and lightly smoking funnel of the gleamingly new steam clipper *Ruapehu*. They each took a deep breath before picking up their bags and walking tremulously up the gangway and on to the deck of their transportation to a new life on the far side of the globe. The 4262-tonne ship had been launched on Clydeside only a few months previously on November 19, 1883, and was now plying a regular passenger route between London and New Zealand.

The ship was built for the New Zealand Shipping Co by J. Elder & Co in one of the Glasgow shipyards where my great-grandfather, Alfred Jabez Berry, plied his trade as a shipwright. There's an enjoyable synchronicity in the thought that he could even have hammered home the rivets that helped hold his eventual relatives by marriage safe on their long voyage.

The 389ft by 46ft *Ruapehu* somehow managed to provide accommodation for eighty passengers in first-class and eighty in second class. A further 250 unfortunate travellers were crammed into the section designated as third class but generally more appropriately referred to as steerage. When all went well – meaning the weather was favourable and the ever-sweating stokers were not slacking with their shoveling – the *Ruapehu* was capable of ploughing along at around 12 knots. This meant the two young women faced the prospect of three months or more of life on the high seas, sharing minimal space and conveniences with their fellow steerage class passengers.

Their fares as assisted migrants were fifteen pounds each, paid by the New Zealand government. The normal steerage class fare ranged from eighteen to twenty pounds and covered all meals 'when the passengers are victualed according to the ordinary diet scale of the ship', according to the July 1849 *Colonization Circular* (No. 9, p. 18). The law required all passenger vessels should have on board enough supplies to provide one pound of bread a day to each adult passenger, and half that quantity for children.

Martha and Mary's voyage took them across the Bay of Biscay to Teneriffe in the Canary Islands and then on to Cape Town before crossing the Indian Ocean to make landfall in Australia at Perth. The *Ruapehu* detoured to Hobart before calling into Melbourne and Sydney and eventually ending its voyage across the Tasman Sea in Auckland.

George Gates was on the quayside to greet his travel-weary sisters. His sturdy arms, muscled from work as a stevedore, hugged them to him in a rough embrace.

'Ay, it's great to see you,' he said. 'Welcome to New Zealand. I hope you like it.'

Martha clung to his arm.

'I'm sure we will. But I'm telling you, no matter what, I reckon we'll be staying. Wild horses wouldn't get us doing that trip again. We haven't had a decent feed for what seems like weeks.'

Mary joined in.

'Yes, it was all right for the nobs up in first class but we haven't seen a bit of meat since we left England. People were looking a lot worse when we got here than when we set out. And some of the goings-on with the crew you'd never believe.'

'Oh yes I would,' laughed George.

'The heat got to everyone,' continued Mary. 'One of the stokers tried to strike an engineer with his shovel and the captain chained the man to the funnel, which was the hottest place on ship.'

'That's nothing,' said George. 'Don't you forget, I've done a few of those voyages meself. Why do you think I jumped ship and did time as a bushman? And I'm not the only one.'

He certainly wasn't. Within a few months of arriving in Totara the girls met another of them, the robust, smiling thirty-year-old Swede Johan Petter Johansson who had braved the waters of Whangaroa harbour rather than spend another day on board a whaling ship commanded by one of the hardest, brutish captains he had known.

As his ship was being towed slowly seawards by its team of whaling boats, Johan nodded to his mates and put his finger to his lips to signal for their silence. He clambered quietly over the gunwales and slipped into the water without a splash. He had a moment of panic; the bundle of tools he had wrapped in oilskin and tied to his waist was weighing him down. And his waterlogged clothes weren't making things any easier. He trod water furiously, anxious not to disturb the surface with his arms. His eyes adjusted to the darkness of the night. Fortunately the moon was hidden behind a heavy blanket of clouds. Soon he was in the wake of his ship and its few lamps were shining on the water further ahead from where he could hear the squeak of the oars in the whaling boats.

As the wavelets from his ship's passing flattened out, Johan levered his legs up to the surface. He extended his arms and began the first of many slow and determined strokes, his eyes focused on a sprinkling of lights shining from a cluster of houses and pubs close to the shore on the far side of the bay from Whangaroa.

Jumping ship was no crime in the eyes of the locals, many of whom had done their time at sea and knew the harsh life it offered. The people of Totara North welcomed Johan into their thriving community, twenty thousand kilometres from his birthplace in a similar waterside town at Umea in the land of the midnight sun. His knowledge of spar making – and the fact he brought his own tools – soon saw him gain employment with timber merchants and shipbuilders Lane and Brown.

Thomas Major Lane and William Brown had established their company only fourteen years earlier but it was soon regarded as the country's leading shipbuilding business using timber wholly cut on the premises – mostly kauri and the harder woods such as puriri and pohutukawa as well as imported blue gum and ironbark. Johan was right at home in the firm's two large sheds where up to sixty men turned out a succession of highly-praised vessels – everything from fleets of small pearlers for the Pacific islands to 350-tonne schooners.

'You think you made the right decision?' the genial William Brown asked Johan one morning as he made one of his regular checks on the work in the sheds.

'Yessir,' replied Johan as he pushed his plane along the length of a spar.

'We're pleased to have you; you're a good worker. A craftsman's hands.'

'Thank you sir.'

'I hear you might be staying.'

Johan paused in his work. He felt awkward. It was a long time since he'd had a boss who talked to him like a friend. The other men often spoke about their two employers in glowing terms and most of them had been there since the yard place had opened. Yet it was still something he found strange. He shuffled his feet and tapped his plane to clear the shavings.

'Settling down, eh?'

Johan stole a look at William Brown. The man was smiling, enjoying the moment. He persisted.

'A young woman fresh out from the old country I believe.'

Johan felt his face reddening beneath his weather-beaten tan.

'Yessir.'

His feet did another involuntary shuffle. He poised his plane ready to continue work then hesitated; he must stand still until his boss had finished talking to him. Every seaman knew insubordination was a punishable offence.

William Brown chuckled.

'Good onya. You'll soon be one of us.'

He nodded towards the length of timber and started to walk on down the shed.

'Don't let me stop you. You'd better get on 'cos we've got a long list of orders waiting … and I expect an invitation to the wedding.'

William Brown and Thomas Lane didn't have to wait long for their invitations. Great-grand-aunt Martha Gates was besotted with her Swedish sailor and within months the pair were married – on 21 February 1885. Almost a year to the day later, on 19 February 1886, Martha gave birth to John Leonard – the first of ten children, five boys and five girls, born over the next thirteen years. By then, her husband was a fully-fledged Kiwi. He was naturalised on 20 May 1885 and changed his name to John Peter Johanson.

Mary matched her sister's speed in the wedding stakes. She was courted by Richard Ward Brighouse and the couple said their vows in front of the Rev S Buchannan at the Wesleyan Methodist Church on 30 July 1885, a year after the sisters' arrival in their new country.

Richard and Mary added four sons and three daughters to the family tree and it is one of Mary and Martha's many Kiwi descendants, Garth Houltham, who made the contact that added so much information to my ancestral searches.

And so, even if I had succeeded in migrating to New Zealand, I would not, as I fondly believed, have been the first in the family to take such a leap into the unknown. Instead I would have merely been following in the footsteps of kinfolk who had taken the same bold step eighty years earlier.

A BRIEF STAY DOWN UNDER

ON a chilly Sunday afternoon, in a leafy and serene back street of inner suburban Melbourne, the past rose up and bit me on the bum.

That's what the pursuit of family history has a tendency to do. So be warned: don't start trawling back through the past unless you are prepared for some shocks and surprises. Skeletons galore lurk in those family closets. Disturb them at your peril.

While undertaking this late-life foray into my family's past I have had to confront abject poverty, rampant infant mortality, dubious bequests, broken marriages, homeless children and grieving widows – nearly all of which seemed to have been neither known nor talked about among recent generations until I went raking over old bones.

As a counterpoint to these murky findings there have been the pleasures of finding many new relations all over the world and of recording my family's dogged upward mobility from terraced slums and mud-brick hovels to middle-class prosperity in suburban villas and rambling rural homesteads on wooded ten-acre blocks.

But this journey back into old Melbourne was something different yet again …

Hand in hand with cousin Lynne I was strolling along Castlemaine Street, Yarraville, an almost secret enclave slowly being gentrified out of its working class origins. We were there to walk in the footsteps of a great grand uncle who suddenly left his native Sussex and inexplicably lived here, 19,000 kilometres from home, for some fifteen years at the end of the 19th century.

For more than 40 years I had lived in Australia believing our little family were pioneers; the first and only members of the Berry line to have landed and settled so far from their deep-sown British roots. Only when delving deeper into the foliage of our tree's rapidly spreading branches did I discover Albert Jesse Britt had preceded us by more than eighty years. And, like us, he had set up home in the suburbs of Melbourne.

The burning question was - why? It is something migrants are continually asked. And which, from my own experience, is a query for which it is almost impossible to provide a concise and definitive response. And here was I posing it yet again to the long-gone and never known Albert Jesse Britt.

Did he, like me, suddenly forsake his family and uproot his wife in a mix of exasperation and hope – dissatisfied with their prospects at home and wildly optimistic about a future on the other side of the world? Maybe this young man shared my deeper unvoiced inner stirrings of domestic discontent and sought salvation on a distant shore – a new beginning in all its many meanings. There had to be strong justification to subject the heavily pregnant Elizabeth to a six-week voyage on a ship that these days most of us wouldn't consider boarding for an excursion around Melbourne's Port Philip Bay.

Until Albert Jesse booked passage on the SS *Orion*, the biggest migration most of the Britts would have essayed would have been from one parish to another or, at most, a few kilometres down the road from Hollington to Hastings. Yet one day in October 1885 he huddled with wife Elizabeth on the dockside at Tilbury as their meagre baggage was loaded aboard the *Orient*, a steamship of a mere 5386 tonnes. The ship had been launched one year previously and was making only its second voyage to the Antipodes.

The Britts faced six weeks of cramped living with some 400 other passengers on a route through the Bay of Biscay, the Suez Canal and the turbulent Southern Ocean. They were leaving in the damp chill of a dark November day to arrive in the humidity and heat of an Australian summer. Christmas would be spent far from family somewhere in the midst of the Indian Ocean.

It was too late for the doubts tumbling around inside Albert Jesse's head. He wrapped a comforting arm around Elizabeth's shoulders and mentally convinced himself they were doing the right thing. Surely anything was better than life toiling as a jobbing carpenter among the building sites and timber yards of Hastings. So much cold and wet. The sunshine and warmth that Australia promised were alone almost enough to justify their move. And the boom times being reported from "Marvellous Melbourne" held far better prospects for their coming child as well as for him and Elizabeth.

Fast forward eighty-four years to a similar scene at London's Victoria Coach Station. For Albert and Elizabeth substitute me, Hazel and Maxine and you have an almost exact replay of the migrant ancestors' doubts, hopes and anxieties. It had been one of those "it sounded like a good idea at the time" moments. At least, that's how it was from my perspective. Maxine, a tot of a mere four years, had no say in the matter and seemed more perplexed than upset or anxious.

Hazel, like Elizabeth, had gone along with her man's extravagantly wishful thinking – that by uprooting themselves from family and friends and transplanting themselves 19,000 kilometres away all their trials and tribulations, personal and professional, would miraculously vanish. And their dreams, such as they were, would be realised. Deeper issues were allowed to lay dormant, never to be discussed, but there were domestic rifts waiting to be healed by this transition to the far side of the world.

Maxine was too young to understand little more than that there was a long journey ahead. However, unlike Albert and Elizabeth's daughter Mabel, she stayed in Australia and quickly adapted to her new country, became a citizen, married and raised two true blue Aussie blokes. Even so there still remain those introspective moments when a glimmer of her Pommie DNA rises to the surface, unerased by fifty years of life Down Under.

Then there is me – wandering down the street where Albert Jesse Britt lived with wife and daughter and pondering on whether I am a latter-day version of this newly-found relative. Did he, too, have to cajole and persuade a doubting and anxious spouse that his madcap plan was all for the best? And did he also have deeper, hidden motives for their migration?

Somehow, in an era long before today's immediate and encyclopedic data resources, he had garnered enough information to persuade himself – if not his wife – that Melbourne (as the city's modern slogan claims) was "the place to be". Or maybe, like me, it was more whim than substance; a running away rather than a pursuit of advancement.

They had married in March, only six months before their ship sailed. There is no knowing whether Elizabeth was pregnant on their wedding day. However, the date of Mabel's birth suggests they wasted no time in getting as up close and intimate as possible. That March had been one of the coldest on record. But once the weather warmed towards summer, people emerged from winter's gloom and escaped the town's narrow streets and cramped houses for a few precious hours in the woodland lanes and bridle paths in the hills above Hastings. The English Channel shimmered in the distance, larks sang and hovered overhead and the gently swaying long grasses offered cover and secrecy for impatient lovers. A romp in the woods and fields of the rolling hills of Sussex Weald would have been as good a way as any for an impecunious couple to spend a balmy spring day. But when the deed was done and the inevitable outcome had fully dawned upon them, the future looked decidedly bleak. As one who had spent more than twenty years living in other people's homes as a domestic servant, Elizabeth had no place of her own and the house in Alfred Street where Albert lived with his parents, brother George and sister Elizabeth had precious little space to spare for one more person let alone the addition of the forthcoming child. And the shed out the back was already occupied by retired gamekeeper Moses Ades.

It was not a cheering prospect.

Over the summer months, as Elizabeth became increasingly aware of the baby growing inside her, the couple spent many hours discussing their future but found little to raise their spirits. For Elizabeth, things were particularly stressful. Although this was her first child, she was ten years older than Alfred and nearing her fortieth birthday – a double burden that she had to carry while continuing her arduous work as a domestic servant. Added to this was the mental strain of adapting to living as part of a family unit again after all those years away from her own folk as a servant in other people's homes. It somewhat dampened the joy of being courted and wed by this dashing young man at a time when she had all but given up hope of being a wife and mother.

Albert did his best to cheer her up and chivvy her into believing "It'll all be right love" – words he did not fully believe yet kept uttering to keep her gloom at bay. She knew he was doing his best and loved him all the more for trying to rally her flagging spirits. But today was different; she sensed a positive mood about him as they threaded their way through the narrow streets close to the harbor. The sea breeze wafted in the smell of frying fish and stallholders spruiked the delights of their plates of cockles, whelks and jellied eels.

'What is it, Albert?'

'I've been thinking, love.'

He was anxious and excited all in one and uncertain how to proceed; unsure of Elizabeth's reaction.

'You're always thinking,' she said. 'Thinking about us, about me and the kid.'

She gave him a gentle dig in the ribs.

'Come on, it's no good keeping thoughts to yerself.'

Albert still felt cautious and tentative. He slowed to a halt and turned and faced her. Elizabeth noticed the frown lines etching his brow.

'We can emigrate,' he blurted out.

Elizabeth stared at him, stunned, not understanding the words. He grabbed her arms.

'Australia,' he said. 'A place called Melbourne. Start a new life. I've been reading all about it. There's plenty o' work. And sunshine. What d'ye say luv?'

For what seemed liked minutes, but was probably only seconds, they stood transfixed, neither speaking, people swirling around them, neither speaking; one waiting for an answer, the other not knowing what to say. Eventually Elizabeth found voice.

'But it's so far away.'

'From what?' asked Albert. 'Y've not been with yer family for years and we'd have each other.'

Albert took Elizabeth's hands in his, gripping hard in his excitement.

'It's all happening over there,' he said. 'There's been a gold rush and everything's happening. The papers are calling it 'Marvellous Melbourne' and saying it's as great as any of the cities in Europe or America, even London. Great tall buildings, offices, coffee palaces, everything. They held the World's Fair there two years back and there's building going on all over the place.'

He paused to gather breath and rummage in his jacket pockets. He pulled out a cluster of newspaper clippings and thrust them at her.

'Look at these,' he implored. 'That's the Royal Exhibition Building, where they held the fair, and these tell how the population has doubled in just ten years. They're desperate for people like me; builders, carpenters, people for work.'

Elizabeth glanced briefly at the pieces of paper. It was too much to take in. He had overwhelmed her with his ideas and his excitement.

'I'll read 'em later,' she said. 'Just tell me what y've got in mind to do.'

Gradually Albert revealed how he had been making enquiries, asking questions and even writing letters. His initial caution evaporated as he told Elizabeth all he had been doing and what he had found out. His enthusiasm was palpable, infectious. Slowly she warmed to his ideas; they seemed to provide so many answers to their dilemma.

What, she eventually reasoned, had they to lose by packing their bags and sailing to the other side of the world?

And so, a few months later, Albert and Elizabeth became assisted migrants standing on the quayside at Tilbury, tremulously contemplating the next six weeks aboard the SS *Orient* – and what awaited them at journey's end.

They arrived at the height of the Australian summer with the weather as fickle as ever – searing days and nights of near hundred degree heat mingled with sudden cool changes and drenching downpours that sent the water flooding down the poorly drained streets. The roads of the new suburb of Yarraville were unmade and either dusty or muddy. Castlemaine Street, where Albert and Elizabeth found lodgings was split in two by the railway line being hurriedly built to accommodate Melbourne's rapid expansion. Their house was a single-storey weatherboard with a tin roof – an airless hot box that took days to cool down.

Within three months, Elizabeth gave birth to daughter Mabel and they began the hard task of adapting to this strange land and to life as parents far from the comfort and help of family and friends. But it was home: there was plenty of work for an able-bodied carpenter such as Albert and Yarraville was developing as a prosperous community with solid public buildings and a busy village-like centre close at hand.

Within a year or two, however, there was the whiff of change in the air. Businesses were struggling, debts were not being paid, and jobs were becoming harder to find. Rumours fed upon rumours and the euphoria of Marvellous Melbourne began to evaporate.

As one building project after another collapsed and the city's grandiose plans for expansion shrivelled to nought, Albert found less and less work was available. He joined the queues of tradesmen willing to turn their hands to anything but trudged home every night bearing the same sad news.

'Nothing,' he said as slumped down on the battered old sofa left behind by a previous tenant.

Elizabeth cuddled Mabel close to her and stayed silent; she knew there was nothing she could say to ease his dejection. But she did wonder if they would have been any worse off if they had never left Hastings. There had been a couple of letters from home and life there seemed to be going along pretty much as usual. Maybe if she dropped a hint or two ... chose her moment ...

Such caution was hardly necessary. By 1891 the boom was fast turning into bust. Debts were called in and banks shut down. There was panic on the stock exchange and thousands of people were thrown out of work. Homes and savings were lost. Pillars of society were ruined. A few people escaped unscathed but many were plunged into hardship. By the turn of the century, the heady days of rumbustuous, rollicking Melbourne were well and truly over and a far more sober and cautious city stood in its place.

Faced by such hardships, Albert, Elizabeth and Mabel decided the migrant life was not for them. Somehow they scraped together the fare and once more endured several weeks of life on the ocean wave. As Melbourne settled into the twentieth century with new resolve, the Britts settled back into the family home in Alfred Street, Hastings. Albert was back working as a carpenter, daughter Mabel had found employment at the central post office and there was extra money coming in from two boarders, colleagues of Mabel working at the post office as mail sorters.

The house was theirs to enjoy. Mum Sarah had died in 1895; dad John, now a pensioner, had moved to St Leonards with a housekeeper to look after him, and brother George, working as a carman, was boarding with a bricklayer and his family elsewhere in Hastings.

For these would-be migrants, the trip Down Under was now nothing more than a blip on their journey through life. Were they another example of whinging Poms? Or maybe it was a matter of being in the wrong place at the wrong time.

WEAVING THEIR WAY TO THE STATES

MIGRATION is based on optimism – the unflagging belief that there's a far better life "over there", no matter where "there" might be. The grass is greener syndrome infects and inspires all who set sail for another land. Why else would you leave all that is familiar for a life in the great unknown?

Second cousin Robert Newsome, a co-descendant of my 4x great-grandfather, Joshua Newsome, was certainly struck by a hefty dose of optimism when he decided, in May 1892, to sail away to America and take nine-year-old daughter Annie with him. He was convinced their new life on the other side of the Atlantic, three thousand miles away from Dewsbury, would surely take a big turn for the better. After all, what had they got to lose?

Life at home and at work was a hard daily grind and showed no signs of improving. Wages paid by the town's mill-owners were static and even falling. His wife, Elizabeth, had died in the spring of 1889 at the age of only 47. This had left him with four children under 20 to provide for without the money Elizabeth had brought in as a carpet winder. Their housing, like that in most of Dewsbury, was cramped, basic and unsanitary. The future for him and the kids held few cheering prospects.

A visiting journalist had described the streets of the mill towns as 'disgracefully neglected' with some of the small courts and cul-de-sacs reeking with stench and 'the worst sort of abomination'. He wrote of ash-pits and outhouses disgustingly choked, with sewage and slops scattered around, often right at the doorsteps of the overcrowded dwellings. And among all this muck sprawled uncared-for children by the score while 'idle slatternly women lounged by the half-dozen'.

The water supply was impure and inadequate and the state of the roads along which workers made their way to the mills was atrocious. Smoke from the increasing number of mill chimneys was becoming a great and growing nuisance. In some mill towns almost half the deaths were among those aged under five. Many workers never lived to see old age, unlike the gentry whose life expectancy was double that of the lower classes.

Despite the often chill and wet weather outside, the thunderous new machines ensured temperatures inside the poorly ventilated mills were often stifling. Washrooms were mostly non-existent, toilets were few and far between (as few as one for every 34 mill-hands) and the many young child workers were highly susceptible to epidemics.

On the plus side was the fact that some of the mills actually provided a cleaner and healthier atmosphere than many employees had at home. Although this was more out of concern for the condition of the final product than for the workers making it, it did mean that in those mills turning out finer grade textiles – sometimes referred to as "stuff" – there was far better lighting and ventilation than in the miserable dwellings the workers returned to at the end of their 10 and 12 hour shifts.

The workers were mostly female and many were very young. They were the mainstay of the weaving, carding, drawing and spinning departments with a ratio of about a dozen women, boys and girls for every adult male. The children spent half their day toiling in the mills and the other half at school; and Annie Newsome would soon be following that inevitable routine. Annie was still at school but Robert knew it wouldn't be long before she would be expected to put in a morning shift as a rag picker or sweeper or some other physically draining task in the stifling, noisy vastness of one of the local mills.

Little wonder, therefore, that Robert Newsome listened with growing interest to talk around the looms and in the public bar at his local pub, the Brighton Arms, of boom times in the mill towns of America. There were many reports of those who had already packed their bags and sailed away and the seed of interest they sowed in Robert's mind slowly matured into a fully-fledged determination. Eventually, all that was holding him back from joining the emigrant trail were concerns for what remained of his family.

The least of his worries was eldest daughter Mary Sarah. After enduring the stifling drudgery of work as a mill hand since she was fourteen, she had escaped into the arms of bootmaker Thomas Dobson and was now five years married with two daughters of her own to worry about. His only son, John, had suffered the usual daily childhood grind in the mills during his schooldays and had begun making his way as a carpet weaver.

Robert's main concerns, therefore, were for 17-year-old Elizabeth and eight-year-old Annie. Elizabeth was already working and bringing in a few shillings a week. But Annie, like so many of Dewsbury's children, was already sickly and malnourished and Robert dreaded what further damage could be inflicted on her frail physique.

In the end, it was an easy decision to make but he was nonetheless tentative as he sat them all down around the kitchen table on a damp and chill February night.

He clasped his mug of tea between his hands and kept his eyes cast down at the table, not wanting to give a hint of his own feelings by as much as a glance or a smile. He plunged in, true to the blunt Yorkshire manner.

'I reckon we should pack up and start over,' he said.

He heard the gasps and sharp intake of breath. A long silence. Elizabeth was the first to speak.

'What d'ya mean ... start over ... where ... how?'

Robert looked up and was relieved to see none of the signs of anger or doubt he had so feared; merely puzzlement and surprise. He dropped his next bombshell.

'America. There's jobs there. A new life.'

Suddenly there was a babble of voices, everyone speaking at once.

'What, all of us?' asked Elizabeth.

'What about Harriet?' said John, raising an issue Robert had already worried about.

'What's America?' chimed in Annie.

Robert made calming movements with his hand and called for quiet. The excitement in the tiny dark room was palpable, even from dour and taciturn John, and it was a real delight to see the way the girls' faces had lit up at his news, even if Annie didn't quite understand what was going on. Her question was the easiest to deal with.

'America is a country a long way away and we would get there on a big boat,' explained Robert. 'We would live on the boat, like in a house, for six days and sleep and eat there.'

He knew it would be far less exciting than he made it sound but he was pleased to see Annie's eyes open wide in amazement rather than the anxiety he had feared. Annie fell silent; it was all too much to absorb. Robert looked at Elizabeth and John.

'I canna make a decision for you. My own mind's made up. It's for the best: I'm going and I'll take the little 'un with me to make sure she's looked after. Neither of youse can do that and I don't want her ending up in the workhouse.'

Elizabeth and John both had steady work – she as a housekeeper and he as a carpet weaver. Robert had no idea whether they felt as down as he did about their future but he was well aware that John was not only courting young Harriet Leach but had hinted they would be getting married maybe later that year. Migration then would mean disruption to two families.

He pushed his cup away and stood up.

'Reet, I'll be taking Annie off to bed and maybe turn in me'sen. I'll leave ye to talk it over.'

....

A few months later Robert and Annie stood hand-in-hand amid an anxious and unruly throng on the dockside in Liverpool, each clutching a small bag containing their few most valuable, and useful, possessions. They edged their way to the gangplank and had their papers briefly checked by a harried official before joining the seemingly endless line of passengers making their way into the bowels of the Cunard liner *Cephalonia*. The ship had been built ten years earlier in just 300 working days, specifically to handle the endless stream of migrants, mostly Irish, who were determined to find a better life in the USA. Although displacing a mere 5700 tonnes, she carried 200 first-class passengers within her 430ft length and still managed to squeeze in a further 1500 in second-class spaces well below decks.

The bunk beds and dormitory accommodation that were to become Robert and Annie's home for the next six days was scarcely an improvement on the cramped and squalid arrangements they had left behind in Dewsbury. Robert laid a comforting hand on Annie's shoulder and gave a light squeeze.

'Dinna worry, lass,' he assured her. 'It's only for a few days.'

He wished he felt as assured and as calm as he sounded. There was no going back and they had no idea what awaited them when they arrived in Boston at the end of a horrendous crossing of the Atlantic. The food was awful, the air fetid and rank with the stench of sweat and malodorous bodies, and any time on deck meant being buffeted by an icy wind that drilled deep into their thin clothes. They clung close together and kept reminding each other it was only a few days before they stepped ashore into a bright new life.

Robert kept Annie's spirits buoyed by telling her what he knew of their intended new home. He told how Worcester was a much younger, newer city than Dewsbury having only really been settled since 1713 after earlier attempts had been obliterated by wars and battles. It had many big mills and factories, just like Dewsbury, but it was more prosperous, more progressive, more vibrant – or so he hoped – than the town they had left behind.

Worcester was an early pace-setter in the industrial revolution. As early as 1837 the town boasted three cotton mills, eight woollen mills, nine manufactories of woollen machinery, four hat manufactories, two paper mills and countless other firms turning out carpets, cashmere, military uniforms, boots, shoes, paper goods and metal ware. It was also a town that offered economic opportunity to women, with female entrepreneurs well to the fore in the city's commercial life. By 1908 the Royal Worcester Corset Factory had become the largest employer of women in the United States with a female workforce of some 1200.

And it was not only Worcester that was thriving and luring migrants. Surrounding communities were expanding rapidly. At nearby Maynard, one of the buildings at the American Woollen Company's Assabet Mills contained more looms than any other woollen mill in the world and the town's population almost doubled in the decade between 1895 and 1905, with most of the workers – mainly migrants – living in houses owned by the company.

At nearby Salem of witchcraft fame, Thomas Kay's woollen mill was largely the work of a man who was applying the skills he had learned in his teens in Leeds. His apprenticeship programs were turning out competently trained textile workers and supervisors with boss dyers earning as much as $US4.50 a day.

At Uxbridge, the Stanley Woollen Mill not only helped pioneer the blending of wool and cottons and fabrics such as satinet and cashmeres and the use of power looms, but was the first in the US to completely manufacture woollen garments from start to finish.

Amid all this progress and innovation, Robert Newsome found Worcester had one appealing aspect above all other booming manufacturing towns. This was its innovative form of affordable housing known as the three-decker. The houses – designed to provide spacious and comfortable apartments for a homeowner and two tenants – sprung up in their hundreds to cater for the steady influx of workers needed to keep the vast new mills churning out all manner of woollens, cottons, worsteds and yarns. The three-deckers offered safe, stable neighbourhoods and were for factory workers and their extended families.

To Robert and Annie such places seemed like paradise and they wasted no time in letting the folks back home know how much they were enjoying their new life. Within a few months Elizabeth had quit her job as a housekeeper and was on board the *Cephalonia* trying to convince herself that the endless seasickness and the bitter cold of the Atlantic's winter storms would all be worthwhile in the end.

Two years later brother John, now married to Harriet Leach, a worsted feeder from Liversedge, embarked with his wife and their two girls, two-year-old Beatrice and babe-in-arms Alice on the *Cephalonia*'s new sister ship, the *Pavonia*, to reunite most of the family on the far side of the Atlantic. Having paid their own way, John had just £3.15 when the family disembarked in Boston. Soon, however, he was earning a regular wage as a wool dyer and Harriet was pregnant with the first of five more children.

'Probably the best thing we ever did,' said a contented Robert at one of their regular family gatherings. 'But I'll admit I was reet scared at the time.'

Elizabeth certainly wasted little time in settling in to her new surroundings. She was soon being courted by George Hargraves, a fellow migrant who was boarding with Robert at 6 Washburn Street, Worcester, and had a well-paid job as a carpet dyer. He was the son of a Lincolnshire farm labourer who had settled in Massachusetts with his wife and seven children ten years earlier when George was six years old. The romance blossomed and Robert proudly walked Elizabeth down the aisle to be married to George on 27 November 1895. Less than two years later the newlyweds were mourning the death of their first child, baby Robert.

They entered the new century on a happier note with the birth of Annie in June 1900, followed by Ralph in August 1906 and Thomas in September 1912. For a while Robert, still working as a dyer labourer, became a resident grandfather. He eventually scraped together enough to take himself and, his brave companion on his big leap into the great unknown, for a sentimental last visit back to the old country. They returned to Worcester in September 1902, sailing from Liverpool to Boston on the Ivernia, ready for Annie to marry locally born Ralph White. When his working days came to an end in 1905 Robert moved in with Annie and Ralph, happily retired and "living on his own means".

Annie and Ralph went on to have three sons and by 1930 were living in a house then valued at $US3000 – a far cry from the dingy back-to-back terrace home she left behind in Dewsbury. Perhaps she occasionally stopped to wonder what her life might have been if Robert had not made that wild and improbable decision to leave the land of his fathers – and she might, from time to time, even have felt the slight tugs and pangs of the old country messing with her emotions. But henceforth this offshoot of my ancestors was determinedly American and has grown into a huge and abundantly flourishing tree.

FROM FARM TO PULPIT

GRAND-AUNT Edith Clara Britt always thought there was something different about Thomas Creasey. He wasn't like the rest of the village lads. He seemed quieter, not so robust, less active, more inclined to wander off on his own. She reckoned he was maybe a bit shy; something of a dreamer.

Looking back to the 1880s and their childhood days in the Sussex village of Hollington, she wasn't sure when she first began to be especially aware of him. Although their birthdays were only a month apart – his in December and hers in January – he was almost four years older so maybe it was not until her schooldays, and even when she was in her early teens, that he really entered her consciousness.

For a while their paths often crossed, while she was making her way to the girls' school on Battle Road and Thomas was taking the path with the boys heading to their school on Wishing Tree Road. These were brief girlish encounters. Edith and her friends giggled at the studious young man whose eyes were usually firmly focused on a book and certainly anywhere but on them. The more he tried to ignore them, the more they raised their voices with teasing comments and jostled and nudged each other as they passed. Once or twice he heard them call out his name. It was hardly surprising that they knew it. Even though Hollington had grown rapidly in recent years, the population more than doubling in the time since Edith's father was born in 1854, it was still only a small village with a few hundred houses and around 2000 people. Everyone knew everyone else through almost daily contact. Letting this lone boy know they knew his name was childish play and Thomas gradually took it in his stride, even throwing the occasional glimmer of a smile their way.

As Edith grew into her teens her sightings of the earnest young man became less frequent. He seemed to have stopped going to school. When she did see him it was usually in the vicinity of the Methodist chapel where Old Church Lane crossed her route to school along Hollington Old Lane. Others his age, or even much younger, were toiling in the fields or at the brickworks as soon as they reached their teens. But Thomas showed no signs of working, even though there was probably useful employment to be had in the coal yard that his father Elijah ran up at the end of Greenleaf Terrace.

Edith blossomed into womanhood and the giggles and shy looks between them gradually developed into more open acknowledgement of each other's presence – a toss of the head, a fluttering of the eyes, all the early signals of flirtation. Thomas was developing too, moving from youth into manhood, becoming less solemn and more confident, surer of the path he wanted to take.

Early in life he had become enthralled by the surge of Methodism that swept across the countryside as John Wesley launched his alternative to the Church of England. As a boy Thomas had been among the crowd who watched the laying of the foundation stone signalling the start of building the solid stone Methodist Church on Battle Road that served as testimony to the rapid rise of Methodism and its firm hold on the local community.

Hollington's early followers of Wesley's ideals had first come together in the 1820s with meetings in Beauport Cottage, the home of John Starr, at the northern end of Old Church Road. In 1823 Mr Starr convinced the justices to grant him a licence to hold church services in the cottage and within two years enough money had been raised to support the opening of a small Methodist chapel further along the road.

The congregation grew to such an extent that in 1835 a Methodist church was built in Battle Road – facing Old Church Road – at a cost of £80. It was later enlarged thanks to a donation of materials by Alderman Stone but was demolished in 1887 to make way for the more substantial building where Thomas worshipped and which is still there today.

Here, at Sunday school, Thomas had been inspired by stories of Wesley's open air meetings and his encouragement of young men to spread his beliefs. Thomas had met and listened to several of these itinerant, unordained preachers on their frequent travels through the Sussex countryside. He found great appeal in the disciplines Wesley demanded of his followers of "doing no harm and avoiding evil of every kind, doing good of every possible sort and, as far as possible, to all, and attending upon all the ordinances of God".

He wanted to be one of these spreaders of the word and in his late teens began discussing his future with local circuit "helpers" and preachers. His parents Elijah (a wonderfully Biblical name that ran through three generations of the family) and Elizabeth were hugely supportive having themselves moved away from the strictures of the Anglican church in which they had been baptised and married to become staunch members of the Hollington Methodists. They subtly encouraged Thomas to broaden his horizons.

'Maybe you should be thinking of getting a job,' said Elijah. 'You'll be needing to talk to people, seeing how they live. You can't be spending all your days studying. The real world's not to be found in a book.'

'Perhaps you could join your brothers,' suggested Elizabeth. 'Mr Wesley didn't spend all his time in the pulpit. He went out into the fields to meet the people.'

Thomas knew there was sense in what his parents said. Like so many other young men in this old rural district his older brothers, Edward and Elijah, were working as agricultural labourers as well as helping their father to cart the coal he delivered to houses in Hollington and beyond. A bit of money in his pocket wouldn't go amiss if he was to travel around the Methodist circuit and pay for board and lodgings.

And so it was that when Edith next saw him in the mid-1890s Thomas was perched high in the driver's seat of a horse-drawn wagon laden with sacks of coal. He took her completely by surprise; he was in neither the attire nor the location she was used to seeing him. For once it was she who was doing the blushing as he politely touched his cloth cap in greeting.

'I haven't seen you for some time,' he said.

'Nor I you,' she stuttered.

He fumbled for something to say.

'Are you still at school?'

'No,' she laughed. 'Can't you see I am too old for that? I am a working girl now – in Hastings as a domestic and living with my grandparents in Old Lane.'

He smiled back, partly at his own gauche remarks for it was quite obvious she was no longer a giggling schoolgirl but a young woman.

'I suppose you'll soon be going back to Hastings?'

'Maybe, maybe not, it all depends ...' Edith replied, surprising herself with the coquettish nature of her response.

Thomas bravely took the bait and they shyly agreed to meet again. And so began a relationship that lasted some fifty-five years and saw my great-aunt make several trans-Atlantic voyages before she and Thomas settled among the small church-going communities of rural Vermont.

Their first meetings were brief and rushed, dictated by Edith's days off and restricted by her need to travel from and to Hastings which, although only a couple of miles walk away, ate into their time together, especially when the weather turned bad.

Thomas was soon talking to her earnestly about his plans to enter the Methodist ministry and although Edith found his enthusiasm infectious she did have concerns about one aspect of a preacher's life. By voicing them, she knew she would be revealing the way she felt about their relationship.

'Does this mean you won't be staying in Hollington?' she asked.

He noted the undertone to her question but let it pass. That was something for later.

'I have to be accepted first,' he said. 'And even after that Hollington will probably still be my base But Wesley always believed preachers become more efficient if they keep on the move so no doubt the officers will be moving me around the Hastings circuit from time to time.'

In early 1896 Thomas Creasey entered the records of the Hastings Methodist Circuit Plan by being listed as a local preacher on trial.

'They have accepted me as an exhorter,' he excitedly informed his parents. He could hardly wait to tell Edith. She was pleased for him and puzzled at the same time.

'What's it mean – an exhorter? It sounds something terrible.'

Thomas laughed at her confusion.

'It's good, not bad at all,' he said. 'It means I've passed an examination on biblical knowledge and the policy of the Methodist Church. It's the first step in a career as a minister. It's a sort of local licence.'

Thomas explained he had not been ordained, nor was he yet one of the church's "travelling" ministers. His role was like that of an evangelist whose main role was to "exhort" people to give their lives to Christ. He was able, however, to conduct services and to preach under the direction of the minister assigned to his circuit.

'And what now?' asked Edith.

'I will conduct services in Hollington whenever I can and continue studying so that I can take the examinations to become an ordained preacher, permitted to conduct the sacraments.'

He had other plans, too, and quietly voiced them in the firm positive tone he had developed as he went about the village "exhorting" people to see the silver lining in every cloud, encouraging them to feel good about themselves and to be hopeful about the future. Edith listened meekly, containing the inner joy his words were bringing.

When Thomas finished speaking she happily agreed to everything he had said. She had hoped for nothing less and on April 16, 1898, walked with her father, my great-grandfather, Stephen Frank Britt, down the aisle of Hollington's ancient Church in the Wood to be married by the rector, the Reverend T W Adam to this dedicated young man. Her bridesmaids were her younger sisters Lucy and Catherine, my grandmother.

Edith and Thomas started married life in rented rooms at the Post Office in nearby Crowhurst, a low-lying hamlet that had existed since the year 774 and yet had never grown much beyond the church, the manor house, two pubs and a population of about 500. Next door were the cottages belonging to the mill responsible for making some of the finest gunpowder in Europe. The mill stream that rippled past their back door, and had Edith in constant fear of rising waters flooding their floors, is these days a feature of local rambles. The post office became a convenience store and the powder mill is today the setting for a country house hotel much favoured by wedding parties.

Thomas continued working as a general labourer while studying for his exams. He also attended meetings of the local preachers on the Hastings circuit and used his spare time to preach and spread the Methodist word.

Eventually all his dedication and study paid off. In December 1898, two circuit officers, Mr Atkins and Mr Reed, proposed and seconded that after successfully undergoing an intensive theological examination Thomas be "unanimously received on full plan".

'It's no longer Mr Creasey but the Reverend Thomas Creasey,' he proudly announced as he embraced Edith with the news. 'I am an ordained minister.'

She hugged him to her, proud of his achievement. She, too, had news to break: the village midwife had confirmed she was expecting their first child and on December 5, 1899, she gave birth to Eva Elizabeth, who not only arrived in time for the new century but also lived right through into the next and died in the US, never having married, on January 12, 2001 at the age of 101.

The following months brought the bitter cold and seeping damp of winter. This, added to the broken sleep caused by the needs of newborn Eva, the draining effect of physical labour and the extra hours demanded by his preaching duties took a heavy toll on Thomas. After one of the wettest Februarys England had known he reluctantly asked the circuit officers to relieve him of some of his duties. He was excused for the whole first quarter of that year and attended none of the regular meetings.

The break worked. By the next quarter and with some pleasant spring weather, Thomas was once more an active participant in church affairs, attending meetings and reporting on lay preachers and visiting missions. He was now a leader at Hollington, responsible for its 36 church members while continuing his day job as a farm labourer. But he had broader horizons in view; he felt he was nearing the end of his time in this small corner of Sussex. He had learnt his trade, as it were, and thought often of how Wesley had urged his followers to step out into the community and to keep moving on as they spread his gospel. Eventually he revealed his thoughts to Edith. But not too directly.

'There is a need for more ministers in America,' he said.

She looked up from feeding Eva, a slight frown creasing her brow.

'So, that's good isn't it? The church must be growing.'

'It is. But it won't continue if they don't have more leaders.' He paused, hesitant about going on. 'Perhaps ... well, I wondered what you'd feel about going to join them. It would be good experience, a new life and from what I hear they would really welcome us.'

She turned quickly, startled, at first her mouth open but saying nothing.

'Thomas, what are you saying? That we should go to America?'

'Yes.'

'But it's so far away.'

'Not really. People are going to and fro across the Atlantic all the time.

Mr Wesley himself and two presbyters sailed there back in the last century and the church is thriving. It's only a few days away. We could always come back for visits.'

Edith fell silent and looked away, gathering her thoughts. There was another reason the idea of a voyage across the Atlantic appalled her. She had been waiting to be sure before confiding in Thomas but his talk of such a big move compelled her to reveal her secret.

'I think I'm pregnant again,' she said.

Her news, backed up by a surreptitious visit to the local midwife, put paid to any immediate plans Thomas may have had. Instead, on August 1, 1902, he readily welcomed Lucy Mae as a sister for Eva and it was almost four years to the day, in August 1906, before the family sailed from Liverpool on the *Empress of Ireland* to explore the prospects for a new life in America.

They travelled to Vermont, a vibrant centre of Methodism right through to the present day, and were warmly welcomed by the locals. They liked what they saw – a gentle rural community not that much different from their home in the Sussex Weald – but cautiously decided to return home to talk things over with their families and the church.

Never one to rush his decisions, yet firmly excited by what the future could bring, Thomas took Eva and their two girls back across the Atlantic in 1909 to the tiny but historic town of Alburg in Grand Isle, Vermont. Here he began work as a clergyman, serving a community with a population that even today struggles to exceed 2000.

It was here, on April 12, 1910, that their third and last child was born – another daughter, named Myrle Kathleen. And so our family tree, with its roots firmly planted in Wales, Yorkshire and Sussex, accepted a graft from which grew a thriving American offshoot. But not before the entire family made one more holiday trip back to Hollington in 1912 to show off new arrival Myrle.

They stayed at the family home at 1 Willow Cottages in Old Church

Road, Hollington, where Thomas's unmarried sister Agnes was living as housekeeper to their widowed father Elijah. Between visits to relatives Thomas found time to conduct services at the local church and on one occasion had the unfortunate experience of seeing one member of the congregation, Thomas Waters, collapse and die.

'It was quite a shock,' he admitted later to Edith. 'But he went in peace and without pain.'

The homecoming had other moments of sadness as Thomas and Edith knew this was a final farewell to many of their family and friends, and especially Elijah, who at the age of 84, was ailing.

'I doubt he'll see out the year,' confided Agnes. And although her father almost proved her wrong, her words proved prophetic as Elijah died at home on December 30. That he left an estate worth more than £1100 was testimony to the solid nature of his business. Thomas and his family had returned to America three months previously having fortuitously changed the family's booking from the ill-fated *Titanic* to one on board the steamship *Royal George* which took them directly into the more convenient Boston rather than New York.

When the family departed from Bristol in steerage class in mid-October it was the last time Thomas, Eva and Lucy would see their native land. Eva worked as a telephone operator, never married and died of old age in the Gary Nursing Home, Montpelier, on January 12, 2001, at the age of 101. Lucy married a Mr Funk and died in Washington, Vermont, on March 5, 1973 at the age of 70.

Edith and Myrle, however, made one more visit to Sussex. They arrived in Southampton on the *Empress of Scotland* in June 1922 to be with the family for the final days of Edith's mother, Clara – my great-grandmother. Clara died within a few weeks of their arrival and was buried in Hollington churchyard on July 22.

It was when the family gathered for the funeral that my mother, then Marjorie Newsome, first met her cousin Myrle. As two young girls in a crowd of grown-ups at such a sombre occasion they were naturally drawn to each other. Both were born in 1910 and only five months separated them.

'Will you be my pen-friend?' Marjorie asked Myrle.

'I was going to ask you the same,' was the excited reply.

From this exchange grew a friendship that spanned the Atlantic for more than seventy years with letters, postcards and photographs documenting their school years, boyfriends, marriages, children and careers. It was random and spasmodic but survived a world war and my parents' numerous shifts of abode – a friendship that endured through the arduous application of pen and ink rather than the instant messaging of today's Facebook and Twitter correspondents.

True to her Wesleyan upbringing, Myrle graduated from the Methodist Montpelier Seminary. With her eventual husband, Abraham Sowma, she went on to run one of Montpelier's most successful hotels and restaurants, the Sowma Motel and Brown Derby Supper Club, eventually dying in 2009 one year short of her centenary.

And so, from the very humble beginnings of a Sussex agricultural labourer and a woman whose mother was confined to the workhouse, our family tree rambles off to the northeastern corner of America to become entwined in those of the Creseys, Funks, Sowmas and doubtless many others.

THE MEN WHO WENT TO WAR

DEATH IN A FOREIGN FIELD

THROUGHOUT years of being a bystander at Armistice Day commemorations and the solemn ceremonies of Anzac Day I found it increasingly unbelievable that I had no connection to the many that had fallen in the wars of the twentieth century. There had never been the slightest whisper of a relative who had failed to return or a hint of families who had mourned the loss of men too young to be sent to war. There was not even some distant cousin or uncle who had been among the fortunate few who had survived the horrors of the Somme or Ypres or Flanders.

The closest association with military men was my father's staunch membership of Dad's Army – the Home Guard – during our World War II sojourn in Fleetwood. He proudly rose to the rank of lieutenant, polished his boots and buckles to a mirror shine before each weekly parade and kept his rifle ever ready to fight the Hun.

Apart from this display of home-front bravado, the Berrys and Newsomes and all their offshoots seemed to deny the oft-repeated statement that no family was left untouched by the twentieth century's great conflicts. Little wonder that I suffered annual tinges of guilt that my line was left unscathed when all others suffered multiple losses and so many other family trees had thriving branches lopped off in their prime.

It was therefore with a perverse sort of relief that I found grand-uncle

Edwin Berry had been killed in action on the infamous Flanders fields on July 26, 1917. He met his death in the massive push forward that culminated in the battle for Passchendaele, one of the great turning points in the thrust for an Allied victory.

This was attrition warfare at its very worst. The summer of 1917 was unusually cold and wet. Much of the fighting was waged in the thick mud of reclaimed marshland that was swampy even without rain. The land had been churned up by heavy artillery bombardment from both sides and even the occasional dry spells did little to lessen the sheer misery of the troops' daily grind. Even tanks became bogged in the endless mud and soldiers often drowned in it.

One can only imagine the atrocious conditions faced by Edwin and his mates as they huddled in their dugouts beneath the German bombardment. How often he must have yearned to be back home with his father and his brothers, Norman and Wilfred, in their comfortable terrace cottage overlooking the vast spread of Milford Haven's harbour. Maybe he even saw the irony in the fact that they lived in Military Road – a daily reminder of how far he now was from his life as a joiner and carpenter down the hillside in Pembroke Dock.

There is nothing to explain what happened to Edwin on that fateful day in July 1917. Whether his death was painful and lingering or blessedly sudden we will never know.

All we have is the stark official announcement that he was "killed in action". That, and a simple headstone among the almost 2000 burials and commemorations of the World War contained in the Guemappe British Cemetery in the French village of Wancourt, about eight kilometres southeast of Arras.

Here lies grand-uncle Edwin ... and I have a framed picture of his headstone to remember him by.

AMID THE MUD OF THE SOMME

IT was a slightly better war for a grand uncle on the maternal side of the family tree. Harold Newsome was 21 years of age when, in 1916, he signed the papers for what was optimistically defined as Short Duration Military Service.

Harold, a cloth finisher in one of Dewsbury's woollen mills, was the youngest son of Jonathan and Elizabeth and brother of my grandfather, Herbert. He served king and country for precisely one year and 159 days before being invalided out as a result of a gunshot wound to his left hand while on active service in France. His battlefield time with the British Expeditionary Force – as the army was then known – may have been a mere 97 days but it spanned some the bloodiest and most disastrous fighting Allied soldiers have ever experienced.

Harold and his mates in the West Riding Regiment arrived shortly before July 1 – later defined as the infamous middle day of the middle year of the war, a day forever to be remembered as the start of the Battle of the Somme and a symbol, if ever one was needed, of the futility of war. It is now etched deep into military history as the British army's bloodiest day. Of the 57,470 casualties, 19,240 were killed or died of their wounds.

Like so many of those around him, Harold was young, keen and up for a fight – and buoyed by the false optimism of those who urged them on. They sang jingoistic songs, jollied each other along with boasts of having the Hun on the run and talked of being back home by Christmas.

'Let's get up and at 'em,' said Harold as they puffed on cigarettes while waiting for orders to proceed.

Ahead lay fences of barbed wire to be cut and crawled through and a terrifying no man's land to be crossed. Above them rained an almost ceaseless barrage of shells from the nearby enemy lines. Hand to hand combat was inevitable. But the tough streetwise young men of the industrial north viewed it all with a false bravado as they soaked up the stirring words of their commanders and felt the ground shudder beneath the poundings of 1500 guns as the artillery began an eight-day bombardment of the German lines.

'That should soften Jerry up,' said Harold. 'Won't be anything left for us to do.'

'Yeah, we'll be able to walk in and round the buggers up,' agreed the man next to him. 'The CO reckons this'll wipe out the Hun's defences and we can stroll through that bloody No Man's Land. The whisper is that the sappers have already laid an underground network of telephone cables up forward for the officers to call back to keep the guns on target as we move in.'

Harold's colleague was spot on with his news. It was the commanders and planners who got things wrong. Very wrong. But in early July they had little idea of what awaited them on the other side of No Man's Land.

The trenches were awash with optimism as Harold tipped his tin hat back at a jaunty angle. He sat on a mound of earth with mates from the 8th Battalion of the King's Own Yorkshire Light Infantry as they listened to their commander's pre-battle speech.

'When you go over the top, you can slope arms, light up your pipes and cigarettes, and march all the way to Pozieres before meeting any live Germans,' the officer assured them.

Harold, along with the rest of them, believed every word.

Within days, all such trust had vanished. On the first day of their supposed advance, the 8th battalion alone suffered 539 casualties as the entire British infantry were mown down by German machineguns. It was the start of four and a half months of endless advance and retreat over patches of ground won and lost and regained. And Harold was in the thick of it.

Flawed tactics weren't helped by individual commanders making their own decisions. Many units moved out into no-man's-land before zero hour so that they could rush the German trenches as soon as the barrage lifted. Sometimes it worked, but for many units the result was disastrous. Much depended on how well the wire had been cut, the intensity of the German defensive barrage and how quickly the enemy could swing their machine guns into action.

Twenty-seven divisions, 750,000 men, went into the attack, of which more than eighty per cent were from the British Expeditionary Force. Ranged against them in the German trenches were a mere 16 divisions of the German Second Army. The odds were stacked heavily in the attacking force's favour.

Unfortunately, the Allies' advance artillery bombardment failed to destroy either the German front line barbed wire or the heavily-built concrete bunkers the Germans had carefully and robustly constructed. Many of the munitions used by the British proved to be duds, so badly made and ineffective that charges failed to go off.

'We're firing blanks,' said a dispirited Harold as the men desperately sought shelter from the hail of German bullets.

'Like me and the missus,' muttered a voice from across the bunker.

'They must've known we was coming,' said Harold.

'Yeah, well eight days of bombing must've given 'em a clue and all the locals have been talking about it for days,' grouched another voice. 'Some surprise that was. Little wonder we're getting nowhere.'

'Yeah, well, I'd rather be back here in me bunker than out there in bloody no-man's-land,' said Harold.

No one argued with that. And for week after week they went back and forth over the same few kilometres of land, hundreds being killed or maimed and neither side gaining any great advantage. Land was captured and lost, villages taken and surrendered. Many troops were killed or wounded the moment they stepped out of the front lines into No Man's Land. Misled by their commanders, hundreds of men laden with supplies and expecting little or no opposition walked slowly towards the German lines and became easy targets for the enemy machine guns.

Because British Commander-in-Chief Douglas Haig was convinced the enemy was on the point of exhaustion and a breakthrough was imminent, the offensive was maintained throughout the summer and into November.

Cold weather and snow rather than an eventual progressive but slow British advance brought the Battle of the Somme to an end on November 18. The Allies had gained 12 kilometres of ground at a cost of an estimated 420,000 British casualties, plus a further 200,000 French casualties.

By then, Harold no longer cared. He had been shot in the left hand, repatriated to Britain and transferred to the Labour Corps where he was eventually assessed as being unfit for combat and "excluded from liability to medical re-examination". The army wanted nothing more to do with him. He was discharged on October 18, 1917, a damaged man no longer needed to fight his country's wars and with no help to pick up the pieces of his old life.

Fortunately sweetheart Lily Bretton, a woollen weaver, was there anxiously awaiting his return and they were married by the vicar, the Rev J J Baldwin, in the parish church at West Town, Dewsbury, on 28 July 1918. Harold obtained work as a warper in the mills and they moved into rooms at 114 Huddersfield Road with Harold's niece Jane, who died there seven years later from the influenza epidemic that swept through the town.

MISSING, AND NEVER SEEN AGAIN

ZOE Berry didn't need to open the envelope the scrawny young telegram boy hurriedly thrust into her hands. She knew instinctively it contained the news every mother dreaded. The boy's frightened face was confirmation enough; he had delivered enough such messages to be aware of their contents and his look told her everything.

'Sorry missus,' the boy mumbled and tipped his cap.

'It's not your fault, lad,' said Zoe. She handed him a penny and he scampered off, glad to be done with one more doom-laden mission.

Zoe shut the door and walked slowly back down the passage and into the shop where cousin Edwin – Zoe's husband – was rearranging tins and packets on the grocery's shelves. He noticed the piece of paper in her hand but was slow to catch on to her slow walk and solemn look.

'What's that then, love? Has the postman been?'

Zoe held the envelope out towards Edwin. Her words were almost a whisper.

'It's one of the boys,' she said. 'You open it; I can't.' Her lips trembled and there was now a quiver in her voice. 'I know what it says.'

Edwin grabbed the telegram and ripped it open. He hastily scanned the brief formal message: "I regret to inform you ..."

His hands shook as he reached out his arms and drew his wife close to him. He held her tight, trying to still her trembling body and calm her sobs. Her voice was almost inaudible.

'Which one is it?'

Edwin squeezed his eyes tight to try to stem the flow of tears; he had to stay strong.

'Cyril,' he said. He felt a shudder go through her.

'My baby boy.'

'Killed in action,' Edwin added, almost as if it mollified the blow.

There was nothing more to say. They had steeled themselves for such a moment for the past two years. As each day ended without the arrival of the dreaded telegram they counted their blessings yet knew, with three sons away at the front, to lose one of them was almost inevitable.

The ringing of the shop's door bell as a customer entered came almost as a relief. They broke off their embrace and wiped away their tears; life had to go on, as they knew it had for so many others up and down the country. Their loss was just one among hundreds of thousands.

Cyril Clarence Berry had been one of the first to enlist, signing up even before his two older brothers, Horace and Percy. Britain had entered the war on August 4, 1914. Its first troops landed in France three days later and Cyril signed his "short service" enlistment papers on August 31. He swore he would be "faithful and bear true allegiance to His Majesty King George the Fifth, his heirs and successors" for a term of three years "unless the war lasts longer than three years, in which case you will be retained until the war is over".

An optimistic hand-written note assured him if, however, the war was over in less than three years he would be discharged "with all convenient speed".

Cyril, an errand boy and grocery assistant in the family shop in Church Lane, Charlton, was all of 19 years and three months old when he committed himself to joining the Middlesex Regiment as an infantryman, knowing full well that within a few weeks he would be shipped across to France to face the full force of the German army.

Like so many of the Berry line, he was slim and slight, a mere eight-and-a-half stone (53.5kg) and 5ft 5in tall and with hardly the build for carrying an infantryman's cumbersome pack and all his weaponry. Having to do this in the mud and slime of the battlefield, and while dodging endless enemy bombardments, became an enormous daily drain on his physical resources. I imagine myself – only marginally heavier and taller than this puny lad, and often castigated for being too thin – coping with what he went through, and I shudder.

Cyril encountered the full brutality of war in February 1915 when he suffered a gunshot wound to his right foot. An abscess developed and he was taken to the field hospital for treatment. He had hardly recovered from this when, four weeks later, he copped another bullet wound, this time in his right thigh and with another abscess developing. This was diagnosed as sufficiently serious to have him sent back to England for proper medical care and a reunion with his distraught family.

As her son's wounds healed and his strength returned, Zoe suffered mixed emotions.

'Sometimes I almost wish his injuries were worse,' she confided to Edwin. 'It would mean he won't have to go back to that terrible war. The better he gets the sooner we'll lose him again.'

It was the best part of a year before her fears were realised. But on Boxing Day, 1915, with General Haig now in command and the disastrous Gallipoli campaign drawing to a close, Cyril was shipped back to rejoin his mates on the front line. Within four weeks of enduring the wet and bone-chilling cold of the French winter, the abscess on his thigh had broken out again and he spent a few days in the field rest station. With the abscess spreading to his groin, Cyril was moved to a hospital at Boulogne and wasn't thrust back into the front line again until late April 1916, weak and frail but deemed fit to fight.

The lull in fighting over the following weeks was intended to dupe the German army into a false sense of security as the British high command began planning what was intended to be a massive push through the enemy lines – the catastrophic campaign that became known as the Battle of the Somme and the biggest list of dead and casualties in British military history.

Cyril went over the top and into the dreaded no-man's-land with thousands of other troops when the battle began on July 1. Eleven days later he was reported as missing. A week after that it was recorded he was to be regarded for official purposes as having died and a telegram was ordered to be sent to the grocery store in Church Lane, Charlton.

It was not until three years later that his mother, Zoe, signed a receipt for the 1914-15 Star and the Victory Medal that were all that remained of his contribution to king and country. His name, however, is commemorated in perpetuity – and "remembered with honour" – at the Commonwealth War Graves Commission Memorial at Thiepval, France.

THE BROTHERS WHO SURVIVED

PERCIVAL Edwin Berry was not to be outdone by younger brother Cyril. Within seven days of Cyril signing on the dotted line, Percival – inevitably known as Percy – had also become an enlisted man, not in the regular army but as one of the much-derided territorials in the County of London Battalion of the London Regiment.

The regiment was first formed as a voluntary force and in 1908 merged with the Yeomanry to form the Territorial Army to regiment the various volunteer battalions in the newly formed county of London. Each battalion had a distinctive uniform and for a long while retained a measure of its original identity, independent of any regular army regiment.

Percy, however – and much to his mother's despair – went one better than Cyril by signing on for four years, not three, although this in reality made little difference as every man who enlisted knew he would be there for the duration. This was certainly true in Percy's case; from the moment he disembarked in France from a troopship that left Southampton on March 15, 1915, he spent his entire army service on the battlefields and it was not until February 1919 that he was discharged with the customary 28 days leave and a £2 advance.

In that time this former shipping office clerk rose through the ranks from private to lance corporal then to corporal, corporal, acting sergeant and finally, in September 1918, full sergeant. His only break from the ardours of war was a couple of sojourns in hospital and two weeks leave back home in England in June 1918.

Eyebrows were raised among medical staff when Percy – as slight and slim as his younger brother – was brought into the field hospital on May 25, 1916. He had all the symptoms of an illness that was causing great debate among the doctors – a frontal headache, dizziness, severe lumbago, a feeling of stiffness down the front of the thighs and severe pains in the legs around the shin area. And, of course, there was the actual fever that had been the initial reason for his collapse. Only a few months earlier medical officer Major J H P Graham had recorded the admission to a casualty clearing station of a private from an infantry regiment who was suffering from "a febrile illness of three days' duration and of sudden onset." It was, he reported, a condition unlike anything he had previously encountered.

Army doctors and pathologists, consulting physicians and clinicians hotly reviewed and debated the growing number of cases showing symptoms like those shown by Percy. The general opinion was that it was a separate and previously unrecognised disease. Its cause was variously attributed to one of the common flies or parasites found in the trenches. One likely culprit was the body louse because the disease was especially prevalent during the winter, when mosquitoes and flies were absent from the trenches. Even the common field vole or mouse was blamed and one doctor suggested it was the result of a rat-derived infection, combined with constipation.

Regardless of the theories as to its origins, it soon earned the label of trench fever and became one of the most significant causes of sickness among the thousands of troops already suffering from the appalling conditions of life in the trenches.

'Don't worry lad, you'll be back with your mates in a few days,' the doctor assured Percy as he lay shivering yet sweating on his stretcher.

Percy wasn't sure whether to be comforted or dismayed by the officer's words. He wanted the fever to end but the prospect of returning to the stench and muck of the trenches was hardly a cheering prospect. But, then, he had his duty to do.

'How long, doc?'

'It's a new one to us, but we're finding the fever dies away within about five days. Full recovery could take up to a month and don't be surprised if it comes back to hit you again later.'

'Sounds just great,' said Percy. 'One dose of this is enough without having to face another dose later.'

The doctor shrugged and moved on; there were far worse cases to deal with than a lance corporal with a fever. Percy closed his eyes and drifted off into another nightmarish sleep. As the doctor had predicted, most of the aches and sweats passed within five days but it was another nine days before he was released to rejoin his unit as they prepared for what was to become known as the Battle of the Somme – the catastrophe that was to take his younger brother's life.

Percy next saw the inside of a hospital three months later when he suffered a bayonet wound to his left hand. This was serious enough to have him removed from the field hospital to the coastal fishing port of Étaples with its notorious base camp and some 16 military hospitals and a convalescent depot. So bad were conditions here, with up to 80,000 men in camp at any one time, that after a couple weeks many of the wounded said they would rather return to the front with unhealed wounds than remain at Étaples. In the winter before Percy's arrival, a mysterious respiratory infection had caused havoc at the base and in 1918 it was the centre of a flu pandemic, or at least provided a significant precursor virus to it.

Writing in his *Collected Letters* (Oxford University Press, 1967), soldier poet Wilfred Owen recalled a stopover in Étaples on his way to the front:

I thought of the very strange look on all the faces in that camp; an incomprehensible look, which a man will never see in England; nor can it be seen in any battle but only in Étaples. It was not despair, or terror, it was more terrible than terror, for it was a blindfold look and without expression, like a dead rabbit's.

Little wonder that in 1917 Étaples was the scene of a four-day mutiny.

Soldiers took control of the camp, held violent demonstrations and disobeyed orders to stand down. It took a corps of machine-gunners to quell the uprising. Three of the mutineers were given ten-year jail sentences, a score more received lesser terms and one, Corporal Jesse Short, was sentenced to death.

Fortunately for Percy, his stay in this vast hospital city was mercifully short – just two days during which he received dressings and antibiotics for his wound before being sent back to his unit. Somehow, apart from a short bout of influenza in July 1918, he managed to stay unscathed and relatively healthy through to the war's end. His superiors recognised his durability and leadership qualities and he rose slowly but steadily through the ranks. When he eventually arrived back at the family grocer shop in Charlton on February 9, 1919, he wore a sergeant's three stripes on his arm and fully deserved the hero's welcome he received, not only from his proud parents and sister Eva – now a blossoming seventeen-year-old – but from all the neighbours.

'And just you wait until tomorrow,' said a joyful Zoe.

Percy threw his mother a puzzled look; war weary and still somewhat shell-shocked, he was already finding it hard to adjust to the sudden change. He had gone from enemy bombardments to the quiet of a suburban street in just a few days; from sleeping in a blanket roll in trenches and bivouacs to slipping between sheets in a comfortable bed. He needed quiet and solitude, not sudden surprises.

'No more celebrations please mum. Let's give it a rest.'

He made a move to escape into the back yard. She held his arm and rushed to explain. 'It's not for you. It's your brother; Horace is on his way home, too.'

Percy stopped in his tracks and a big smile lit up his face.

'There, I knew that would make you happy,' said Zoe.

She didn't know the half of it, thought Percy. His feelings went beyond happiness and relief at knowing Horace was on his way home. It meant he would have someone to talk to who knew the full horrors of what they had both been through.

Horace had been the last of the Berry boys to sign the enlistment papers – a full nine months after Cyril and Percy. He put his name to the forms handed to him by Company Sergeant-Major J McGregor on June 26, 1915, and, much to his surprise, was immediately drafted into the 2/7th battalion of the Gordon Highlanders.

More solid, slightly taller and heavier than his brothers, Horace was the knockabout lad of the family – the one most likely to get into scrapes and earn reprimands from teachers and superiors. He didn't take easily to the rigid discipline of the army – and especially that of the redoubtable highlanders – and occasionally was deprived of his pay as penalty for his offences. Fortunately for him, these misdemeanours did not occur on the battlefield but in the comparative safety of Norfolk where the 2/7th was billeted at the army training camp at Taverham and then at the now demolished Witton Hall, once the estate of Lord Wodehouse, before being disbanded on September 30, 1918.

'It wasn't as if it was me that was hitching a ride,' grumbled Horace, back in his tent after being stopped two days pay. 'The wagon was almost empty and the pack was heavy. I kept on marching.'

His commanding officer, Major Simpson, had failed to share his point of view. He found Horace guilty of carrying his equipment in a transport wagon while on active service and "when in the line of march." His combination of cheek and laziness cost him two days pay.

Others at Tavenham committed more serious offences. It was not uncommon for soldiers to wander off from the tents lined up along the Fakenham Road when they heard they were to be shipped to France. One unfortunate escapee climbed into a high tree in the area known today as Ghost Hills and tied himself with a rope into the upper branches. He tied the knots so tight that he was unable to free himself and eventually died of exposure. His body remained in the tree un-noticed for many months.

'Think I'd rather take my chances against the Hun than end up like that,' said Horace when the news of the man's discovery spread through the tents.

A few weeks later he got his wish with a transfer to the 16th brigade of the Queens Royal Rifles and the 3rd Echelon, the British Expeditionary Force's administrative headquarters in France. Only now, as 1917 was drawing to a close, was Horace about to spend his days and nights hearing the endless thunder of the artillery and come face to face with the enemy.

The second battle of Passchendaele, the culminating and final attack during the third battle of Ypres, was drawing to its close as the Allies fought to gain higher and drier ground before winter set in. The only way troops could be moved up to the front line was by narrow wooden boardwalks laid between the shell-holes. Slipping off the duckboards could be deadly with soldiers often drowning in mud under the weight of their equipment.

Horace had heard stories from returning soldiers and thought he knew what to expect. But nothing had prepared him for the reality. The first thing was the smell - from rotting bodies in shallow graves and from men who hadn't washed in weeks because there were no means of doing so; the stench from overflowing cesspits and the acrid fumes of the creosol or chloride of lime used to stave off the constant threat of disease and infection. Mingling with this was the cordite, the lingering odour of poison gas, rotting sandbags, stagnant mud, cigarette smoke and even cooking food. Like all newcomers, Horace soon got used to the smell and found it mingling with his own body odour. He also learned to accept the presence of the thousands of rats festering the trenches. Gorging themselves on human remains and all the other detritus, they could grow to the size of a cat.

'We've got better chances against the Hun than ever beating these buggers,' said a fellow private as he and Horace dug into their mess tins for yet another feed of bully beef and beans and watched the rats scamper past. 'They breed quicker than we can kill 'em. They're killing us off faster than Jerry's bullets.'

It was no exaggeration; disease and sickness were rampant with much of it due to the rats. Lice were another huge problem and few soldiers escaped unscathed.

Horace had two brief sojourns in the field hospital in August 1918 and four days after being discharged for the second time he was back there again – this time with the same trench fever that Percy had suffered. He was too sick to be treated locally and managed a weak but grateful smile when he heard orders were being issued for him to be evacuated to England.

It meant Horace's war was as good as over. He arrived at the Western General Hospital in Cardiff on September 17, 1918, and stayed there until granted 10 days leave on November 6. By the time his leave ended, the war was over and he had to wait only until February 21 to be finally released into the arms of his welcoming family with £2 in his pocket and the specialist military qualification of signaller – a skill he never felt motivated to use again.

AN EAST AFRICAN DISASTER

FAST forward two decades. The world war that followed the "war to end all wars" was in full swing when second cousin, and Lynne's great uncle, William John Leslie Blair found himself stationed in East Africa and Ethiopia. Here, far from the blitzkrieg going on in Europe, the Allies were battling to hold off Italian forces determined to make inroads into the African continent and control the Suez Canal.

Compared with the young men who had enthusiastically enlisted in World War I (and those brave youths who fought the Battle of Britain earlier in World War II), Les was almost a senior citizen by the time he was sent off to do his bit.

It was his second major conflict. World War I was less than halfway through when he had enlisted as a career soldier straight from Devonport High School at the tender age of 15. As the second oldest of four strapping lads, he revelled in physical activity and so the initial training on Exmoor and Dartmoor was more pleasure than hardship. Stationed with the Duke of Cornwall Light Infantry in Bodmin, he breezed through the demanding physical exercises, testing obstacle courses and long route marches and went on to join the Devonshire Regiment. There his fitness and sporting prowess were eventually recognised and set him on course to become one of the British army's elites as a member of the Army Physical Training Staff.

'No one applies to join the corps,' he proudly told fiancée Gwendoline Bound one day when they were walking out in Bodmin well before their marriage in 1929. 'You are hand-picked and drafted.'

'Why am I not surprised?' said Gwen as much to herself as to Les. 'I'm sure I'm not the only one who thinks you're rather special.'

Much as she admired him, Gwen didn't fully realise quite how special Les had to be to serve with the APTS. But she was well aware of the excitement in his voice as he told her of the many arduous weeks of training he faced before final acceptance into the corps.

'It makes me exhausted just hearing about it,' she said. 'I thought soldiers were fit already without all this extra stuff.'

'Not really' said Les. 'It's not enough for them to be able to fire a rifle or throw a grenade. They have to cross miles of country on foot, often at night and without sleep. There could be hills to climb or perhaps rivers to swim across. And they have to carry packs and equipment. And still be fit enough to attack the enemy.'

Gwen shook her head, part in amazement, part in admiration.

'And that's what you're going to do?'

'More than that,' said Les, relishing the thought. 'We have to be fitter than the men we train.'

Ahead of Les was a physical training instructor's course after which he would return to his unit for continuation training to await selection to attend a 30-week course and, .if successful, become a fully-fledged member of the RAPTC with promotion to sergeant – the lowest rank in the corps.

Right from the corps' inception in 1860, when twelve highly talented individuals aptly known as the Apostles were given the task of improving the army's health and fitness, its members have been regarded as exceptional human beings. The selection process then, as now, is lengthy and extremely demanding, physically and mentally. It can take several years from a soldier's initial selection to the point where they actually join the corps. They have to excel not only in a wide range of physical activities but also in leadership and education. They are also expected to demonstrate tolerance, humour and a well-developed sense of esprit de corps – and to instil these qualities into those they instruct.

What started as a small band of keep-fit instructors has expanded into an elite corps that is responsible for ensuring the country's fighting men and women can cope with the most arduous battlefield conditions and maintain peak fitness in peace as well as war.

Although considerably expanded during World War II it has always been one of the smallest corps in the army. The rapid rundown of staff when hostilities ended in 1919 eventually reduced the APTS to only 150 men worldwide.

The 1920s saw the corps training the British Modern Pentathlon team at its Aldershot HQ and taking a far more scientific and professional approach to physical training. Tough tactics teams were organised to operate in the front line and instructors were posted to the commandos, the parachute regiments and the elite Special Air Services. Training was designed to prepare the troops for battle and many instructors went into action with the men they had trained.

Early in 1935 it was decided that the army and the nation were not as fit as they should be when compared with Germany, Italy and Sweden and the British Medical Association decided the best course of action for the health and fitness of the nation was to follow the example set by the APTS and introduce the use of soldiers' physical training tables and ensure they were carried out.

The start of National Service in 1939 gave a boost to the APTS and by September its strength had increased from 169 men to 280. With the outbreak of war, there came a further increase and by December the same year it totalled 750. Soon it was formed into a fighting unit and on September 16 1940 became the Army Physical Training Corps with many of its members subsequently receiving awards for gallantry or being mentioned in despatches.

Les grew with the corps, rising up through the non-commissioned ranks before being selected for officer training at Sandhurst. He passed out with a commission and went on to help design the commando course used to train troops for the Normandy landings.

By the time he arrived in East Africa in the early 1940s he had attained the rank of major. His domain extended through Kenya, Ethiopia and into the Sudan and Somalia – all places where British troops were deployed.

On the morning of November 29, 1944, Les and six colleagues gathered in the huts that constituted the airport in Juba in South Sudan. The equatorial heat was stifling and draining. Dust and sand from the unmade roads swirled around them. It was a far cry from a wintry Nottingham where Gwen now lived with their daughter, 10-year-old Shirley, anxiously awaiting her husband's return.

'Even Nairobi's better than this,' grouched one of his companions.

'Not long to go now,' Les consoled him. 'At least we're flying there and don't have to trek across the desert.'

They watched as airport staff loaded a BOAC Lockheed Lodestar sitting on the levelled dirt that passed for a runway. None of them could imagine that this would one day be the site of a thriving international airport serving what has become one of the fastest growing cities in the world, despite woeful hygiene, unmade roads, intense poverty and inadequate supplies of water and electricity. The men wiped sweat from their foreheads and shielded their eyes from the dust.

'Three hours to a shower and a beer,' said Victor Hayes-Gratz. The 31-year-old Royal Artillery captain licked his lips at the thought. 'Should be there in time for lunch.'

Les acknowledged his remark with a nod towards a nearby hut and the four men who had just emerged clutching papers and brief cases.

'Looks like things are moving,' said Les.

The pilot, Captain Leslie Davies, his navigator and two radio operators had left the hut and were heading towards the aircraft, its rear low to the ground, its nose pointed skywards.

'Two civvies,' commented another of the waiting group.

Captain Davies and radio officer James Rimmer wore the uniform of BOAC, matching the aircraft's insignia. Navigator Ernest Laughton and the second wireless operator, George Menzies, however, were clearly members of the RAF Volunteer Reserves – Laughton already a warrant officer at the age of 24 and Menzies, a fresh-faced 20-year-old flying officer barely out of flying training school.

'Don't care what uniform they wear as long as they can fly that thing,' replied Hayes-Gratz as ground staff indicated they should start boarding.

There was plenty of room for them to spread out with seven of them, fifteen seats and no other passengers.

Final checks were made, the propellers whirred into life and the plane started a slow trundle down the airstrip ready for take-off on a 803km southeasterly route over mostly uninhabited bushland, forests and several mountain ranges rising well over 12,000 feet.

Les and his team tried their best to relax amid the noise of the engines, the buffeting from the wind and the frequent drops into air pockets. They were well into the flight and becoming used to the discomfort when disaster struck. About twenty minutes out from Nairobi and with the crew starting to plot their final approach into the destination, the Lodestar ploughed into the unyielding slopes of the Aberdare Ranges. The deaths of all on board were later declared to have been instantaneous.

All radio contact was lost. RAF and BOAC aircraft were sent to search the area but nothing was sighted. It was not until two locals reported what appeared to be wreckage eight miles away in a peak of the Aberdare Ranges that another RAF plane was able to identify wreckage at an altitude of 12,000 feet on the north side of the highest peak, about 80 miles from Nairobi and one mile west of the mountain known as the Sleeping Warrier.

Investigators had to make a 12-mile trek from their base camp to reach the crash site. The harsh terrain and thick bush made it impractical to recover the bodies; they were interred on January 5, 1945, close to the scene at a location overlooking a valley. The burial was carried out with full military ceremony by military personnel and BOAC officials. On January 14, eleven crosses and a wreath were placed on the grave by the Imperial War Graves Commission.

It was only later that the eleven victims were brought down the mountain. On November 20 1945 they were given a full military burial in the Nairobi War Cemetery where cousin Leslie Blair now rests in perpetuity in grave 2C24.

On September 18 1948, a memorial service was held for 26 members of the Army Physical Training Corps, including Les, at which a memorial tablet was unveiled in their honour by Field Marshal Viscount Montgomery of Alamein whose words "fighting fit and fit to fight" had been adopted as the corps' motto.

Les went against family tradition by joining the army as the majority of the family were connected to the sea, either as shipwrights, Customs officers or Royal Navy officers. Les's father, Peter, joined the navy on his twenty-eighth birthday in 1896 and his oldest brother, Charles Owen Blair, Lynne's grandfather, volunteered in 1914 at the age of 15. While at sea during WW2, Charlie jumped overboard and saved a Russian sailor from drowning. He was awarded the DSC and was subsequently promoted to lieutenant commander. The Russian sailor presented him with a set of silver napkin rings.

STRANGERS ON THE DOORSTEP

As the clock ticked over from the 1800s and into the twentieth century, my great-grandparents, Elizabeth and Jonathan Newsome, answered the knock on the door of their dingy terraced home in Dewsbury's grandly named but impoverished Hanover Square to admit the dark "stranger" standing there wrapped up against the bitter cold.

In reality the stranger was no such thing but Jimmy Beaumont, a neighbour from a few doors down, who stood on the doorstep thrusting towards Jonathan a lump of coal held in one extended hand.

'And here's your tot,' he grinned as he brought his other hand from behind his back clutching a small glass and offered it to Jonathan.

'A happy new year to you.'

Jonathan accepted the piece of coal and took hold of the glass. He took a slow appreciative sip of the whisky, letting it roll around his mouth, and handed back the glass.

'Aye, and the same to you Jimmy. One can only hope things will get better.'

He stood aside and ushered Jimmy inside.

'Stop awhile and have a bite. Lizzie's made the shortbread.'

It was all part of a traditional ritual that had gone on for centuries in Britain's north. Each new year was welcomed with a "first footing" whereby the first person allowed across the threshold after the clock struck midnight had to be a dark-haired visitor bearing whisky and a symbolic piece of coal plus shortbread, salt and a black bun. A fair-haired visitor signified bad luck. I can well recall, when we lived "up north" in Fleetwood, being kept up well beyond my bedtime so that I could be urged out into the freezing night to become the harbinger of another year and be the first to foot it into our house, a lump of coal in hand.

For Elizabeth and Jonathan there was little to celebrate; they could see little prospect of the daily struggle changing, of there being more money in the kitty, better job prospects or an improvement in their living conditions. Five of their six children were still living at home and they were also treating seven-year-old Jane as their own child rather than as the grandchild she really was.

It had been an easy decision to make when, at the age of 15, Alice had informed them that she was pregnant. The father was John Fell, who was not much older than Alice and, in Elizabeth's view, definitely not cut out to be a husband at that young age even if he was already doing a full day's hard toil as a cloth finisher. So there was nothing to do but take in the child they had named Jane and bring her up as one of their own. And even when Alice and John did tie the knot some time later in September 1899 Jane remained with Elizabeth and Jonathan while her parents set up home a few doors away at 3 Back Hanover Square, accommodation they later shared with John's brother William and his wife Annie.

The only offspring not still living at home that New Year's Eve was Joseph, their eldest child, who was boarding with heavily pregnant wife Sarah Ann and year-old Harold a short walk away at 18 Kent Street. Sarah gave birth to Herbert a month into the new century but less than a year later she and Joseph were mourning his painful death from convulsions brought on by the cutting of his teeth – a now little known cause of death known as dentition.

The distraught parents could do little but watch and try to swab away the fever as little Herbert writhed in pain, unable to sleep or ingest the simplest of food, his mouth frothing, eyeballs rolling and his tiny body racked with convulsions.

He was one more victim of the poor hygiene and sanitation still prevalent in our overcrowded industrial centres at that time. It was so easy for infants being weaned at the time of teething to encounter contaminated milk or food. Harold was far from alone in his early death: to scroll through the birth and death records for late 1890s and early 1900s is to reveal a long succession of children who died within months of being born.

To John and Elizabeth their grandson's death was simply one more tragic event typical of the lives they and all those around them daily endured. Little wonder that they saw little cause for excessive celebration when the first footers came knocking each New Year's Eve. Bluff Yorkshire pragmatism and the realities of life tended to blunt any show of optimism.

But at least they celebrated on Christmas Day 1901 when the family gathered at St John the Evangelist Church in Dewsbury Moor for the marriage of daughter Emily, my grand aunt, to Percy Wray, a fellow mill worker from down the hill by the river at Ravensthorpe. And there were further celebrations in the following year, first in March when Emily presented them with grandson Edmund and again on May 17 when they returned to St John the Evangelist to witness pregnant daughter Edith marry coal miner George Alfred Gott in time for the birth of son Wilfred in October.

It was around this time that Herbert, the second of Elizabeth and Jonathan's four sons – and eventually my grandfather –understandably rebelled against the atrocious conditions he faced as a 15-year-old piecer in the woollen mills and did what few Yorkshiremen would seriously consider and headed to the soft southern counties. There he somehow not only ended up working in HM Dockyard at Chatham as a labourer and electrician but, equally inexplicably, also met and wooed the good-looking Catherine Britt, a lass nine months his senior who was working as a domestic servant in Hastings. Herbert was a month away from his eighteenth birthday when he and Catherine walked down the aisle at the

Church in the Wood, Hollington, on August 3, 1903.

Meanwhile, back in Dewsbury, Herbert's sister Emily and husband Percy were well on their way to producing another grandson for Elizabeth and Jonathan. Percy Ivan arrived in March 1904 but once again the family's joy was comparatively short-lived. In April 1907, Percy senior succumbed to heart failure after eight days of pneumonia and John and Elizabeth found themselves not only providing their daughter and her two sons with a home but also looking after the boys while Emily went back to work as a comb feeder at the mills.

But at least they had some help as Jane, the granddaughter they called a daughter, remained at home, too sickly to undertake the hard physical labour most working women had to endure. They also saw the arrival of more grandchildren via Joseph and Sarah. Undeterred by the tragic death of baby Herbert, Sarah remained almost permanently pregnant, giving birth to eight more children (and thus eight more cousins for me) over the next thirteen years.

By then the "war to end all wars" had well and truly begun and more and more young men were lining up at recruiting offices keen to do their bit for king and country. Eventually, as the bitter conflict dragged on, there were few families left untouched by death or injury. Many were faced with making huge adjustments as they adapted to life without husbands and fathers or tried to cope with former breadwinners who had been cast on to the unemployment scrap heap, shell-shocked, gassed and maimed.

Jonathan and Elizabeth were among the fortunate ones, with their three surviving sons coming through almost unscathed, Herbert, my grandfather, did his bit working on the navy's warships in HM Dockyard at Chatham, Edmund proved too old for military service and Harold was invalided out after receiving a gunshot wound to his arm on the Western Front in France.

Sadly, however, my great-grandparents didn't need a war to bring untimely death to their doorstep. Hostilities were barely a year old when they were rocked by the sudden death, at the age of 39, of daughter Alice.

'She just passed out,' said her distraught husband. 'It was as if she had a fainting fit.'

Dr James Ashby nodded sagely and gave John a sympathetic look.

'It was much more than that,' he said. 'It was her heart that gave up. She was not a healthy woman. The heart stopped pumping blood through her brain and that's what you thought was a fainting fit.'

The words he wrote on the death certificate were more explicit. Alice had died as a result of a fatty degeneration of her heart. For a long time she had been subject to giddiness, headaches and chest pains. Dr Ashby had done his best but knew there was no real cure apart from rest and a light meat-free diet. Alice was an invalid and her life would inevitably be cut short.

A bitter Elizabeth was somewhat harsher in her judgment.

'It was a marriage cursed from the start,' she declared to her husband, the memory of Alice's childhood pregnancy still strong in her mind.

She had grudgingly accepted Alice's eventual marriage to the child's father, John Fell, but as they both seemed content to leave their daughter's upbringing to she and Jonathan, there was scant regard in her soul for either of them. She could not, however, deny her maternal feelings at Alice's passing and mourned her death with the rest of the family. However, her low regard for John Fell remained and she felt fully vindicated when she heard, two years after Alice's death, that he had married Julie Annie Athey, a widow with seven children and three years his senior.

'More fool her,' scoffed Elizabeth as she digested the news. 'I see they got married on April Fool's Day. That'd be right enough.'

Grand-aunt Alice had died at home at 114 Huddersfield Road on February 5, 1916, and fortunately, before more doom and gloom struck the Newsome clan, there was the cheering occasion on July 8 that same year when son Edmund, now 27 and working as a spinner in the woollen mills, married Eleanor Tattersall, also a spinner, in St Matthew's Parish Church.

'Just in time, I'd say,' murmured Elizabeth as her future daughter-in-law walked down the aisle. It was an accurate prediction: Eleanor gave birth to Clifford, the first of the couple's three children, six months later on January 17, 1917, and added further to the cramped conditions at 114 Huddersfield Road, Ravensthorpe, where all three generations were now living close to the river in Dewsbury's mill district.

Before that happy event, however, Jonathan and Elizabeth were hit by another family tragedy with the brutal death of son Joseph in the mines out at Ossett. The *Dewsbury Reporter*'s detailed account on January 1, 1917 of the death and inquest made sad reading and a mournful start to the new year.

The underground accident left daughter-in-law Sarah to bring up a family of six boys and three girls. Elizabeth knew only too well what Sarah had to face, having had ten children of her own and now, late in life, still having to cope with bringing up granddaughter Jane.

But there was little she and Jonathan could do to help Sarah, depending as they did on Jonathan's meagre wage as a rag picker and scavenger. It was only later, towards the end of his working days, that he managed to obtain somewhat more secure and marginally better paid work as a labourer with the local council.

As the fighting dragged on and hundreds of thousands of young men fell to their death in the mud of Flanders, my grandparents enjoyed a glimmer of cheer amid the unremitting gloom that had descended over the country. Their youngest son, Harold, was coming home from the front; the welcome mat and bunting were ready and waiting – and living and sleeping space became an even bigger squeeze in the house on Huddersfield Road.

Harold had enlisted in the Kings Own Yorkshire Light Infantry for short duration military service at the start of 1916. Now, after a year and 159 days of army duty that included 97 days with the British Expeditionary Force in France, he was being discharged. A gunshot wound to his left hand had rendered him unfit for further military service and on October 18, 1917 he was handed his demob papers, a 28-day leave pass and a £2 advance on his pay.

Harold was far more fortunate than many who had seen active service. Although wounded, he could still work and was soon back in the mill as a cloth finisher and earning enough to be able to marry weaver Lily Bretton at the parish church in West Town, Dewsbury, on July 28, 1918. One of those who signed the register as a witness was his "sister" Jane, who had performed the same duty at her "brother" Edmund's wedding two years earlier.

With the coming of Armistice Day on November 11, 1919, the nation heaved a collective and weary sigh of relief and began to count the cost as it struggled to return to something approaching normal life. Lily had moved in with Harold to live with my great-grandparents and Edmund, Eleanor and Clifford and together they battled on through another bitter Yorkshire winter.

Jonathan, at 68, was still trudging off daily to work as a council labourer. There was no early retirement, or superannuation, in those days and it was a matter of keeping going as long as you could. Maybe that is where I got the genes that have enabled me to compete successfully as a distance runner well into my seventies, although my exertions are for some sort of masochistic pleasure and not out of the necessity imposed on Jonathan and thousands like him.

It was the bitter weather and the chill damp living conditions that so often ended lives rather than hard physical toil. This was certainly the case with Elizabeth who succumbed to a severe bout of bronchitis in the winter of 1923, with her son Edmund by her side. Doctor Robert Beattie wrote the certificate confirming her death on January 23 at the age of 70 years. Or was she some years older? It certainly tallies with the copy of her birth certificate now in my possession and with her age as recorded every ten years on the census. Yet a late discovery in my research unearthed a very clear entry in the parish register of Dewsbury All Saints Church showing Elizabeth Frances Hooley (as she then was), daughter of Elizabeth and James, being baptised on July 16, 1845. And an annotation alongside states she was born on June 15, 1845. Such a conflict is far from unusual in genealogical research, especially in the older records, and there is now no way of confirming great-grandmother's true age. Sadly, whatever her age, her death came without Jonathan there to comfort her. He now had troubles of his own.

Although used to hard manual labour all his life, wielding a pick and shovel were taking a daily toll on Jonathan's body; an incurable weariness now assailed his once sturdy frame. Inevitably he began to lose the concentration essential for working with implements. There was a stumble, a fall and the sudden blow of a spade against flesh. Jonathan collapsed, pain etched on his face, one hand reaching down his leg. His workmates removed a boot and revealed a right foot, already swelling, with blood oozing from a deep cut. It was hastily bound in whatever rags and cloths were to hand and a doctor eventually arrived. The next stop for Jonathan, in excruciating pain and weakened by loss of blood, was the Dewsbury Poor Law Union workhouse on Heald's Road.

This grim and solid Victorian pile, set between Staincliffe Mills and Staincliffe Colliery, began life as a refuge for paupers, tramps and the homeless. It accommodated 46 "inmates" supervised by a rheumatic female nurse assisted by pauper servants. Gradually it expanded in size and scope, diminishing the unventilated, foul and unsavoury workhouse aspect while adding separate male and female wards and expanding its nursing staff. Extra wings were added as it changed from a poorhouse into a substantial infirmary with nurses and hospital wards. During the First World War, it was used to accommodate military patients and today is the site of the Dewsbury and District Hospital.

Facilities were basic but much improved on what was provided in the building's early days when Jonathan arrived there as a patient. However, it made little difference. Septicaemia set in, followed by gangrene, and on January 23 1926, exactly three years to the day after Elizabeth's death, great-grandfather Jonathan gasped his last breath. His son-in-law, George Gott, husband of Edith, now living in a more salubrious area at 12 East Parade, was on hand to deal with the paperwork.

And son Herbert, now married to Catherine and father of daughter Marjorie, became my sole living link to the Newsomes of the past.

FISH, AIR RAIDS AND BATH NIGHTS

SOME time between the two world wars, Nan and Gramp Newsome, my maternal grandparents, moved the few streets from their home in Richmond Terrace, Gillingham, to another terrace house at 20 Charter Street from where, in 1933, daughter Marjorie, a drapery shop assistant, left to marry the dashing and handsome young Customs officer Wilfred Berkeley Berry.

Two years later, in the early hours of September 11, a date now infamous the world over, I was pushed out from between my mother's thighs and took my first bawling look at the world from a maternity bed in the Royal Naval Maternity Nursing Home.

Home for the next few years was a tall terrace house in Barnsole Road, Gillingham, where "Bill" (as Dad was forever called) and Marjorie moved after their honeymoon at Folkestone. Here I can recall a long and narrow back garden where I would pedal around on a wooden scooter and play with "Pad Pad" – a gentle, brown long-haired mutt whose correct name was Paddy.

These idyllic days came to an abrupt end with the declaration of war and the first of many postings for Dad that resulted in a move to "foreign" territory – across the great divide between south and north England to Fleetwood, a fishing port wrapped into the broad arms of Morecambe Bay on England's windswept northeast Lancastrian coast.

Today, Fleetwood is probably best known as the home of Fishermen's Friend, the potent lozenge guaranteed to scour your palate dry of all tasting ability while you suck to relieve the cough which they're meant to attack.

Back then, as the country's third largest fishing port, it was not only a prime source of marine food but also a vital link in the nation's seaborne defences.

IT was Christmas, 1943. I was in hospital recovering from acute appendicitis and the removal of the offending organ. Earlier I had kicked and screamed resistance when the paramedics arrived but it only took one of them a matter of seconds to wrap me in a blanket and carry me downstairs and into the ambulance.

Although only a skinny runt of a kid, I was accorded grown-up status at Fleetwood Hospital and moved out of the children's ward to lie in a post-operative daze alongside men with far more chronic conditions than mine. While they coughed, wheezed and groaned I hid my embarrassment at chundering into the enamel bowl at my bedside by keeping it as quiet as possible. Many of my fellow patients would have been victims of the harsh life lived by the local trawlermen and by others engaged in protecting the country from a determined aggressor.

Britain was halfway through the Second World War and the nation's stiff upper lip was being seriously challenged by food shortages, nightly air raids and the sinister 'doodlebugs' (unmanned aerial devices that turned into bombs the moment their engines cut out).

The life of a Fleetwood trawlerman was extremely hard. As local historian Alan Duggan has written it was almost impossible to visualise what the fishermen had to endure; yet endure it they did, without a second thought. As Duggan comments, it was just a part of the job and it had to be done. He records that life on board left little room for the niceties of life that others took so much for granted. The crew's only luxury was the chance to close their eyes and snatch a few moments sleep.

Forecastle accommodation was very cramped and Spartan with tiers of bunks at either side of the tapering compartment, and a mess table in between. Often, the deckhead was not much higher than six feet, meaning that the taller members of the crew had to stoop to avoid the risk of braining themselves. In this space, usually heated by no more than a small and inadequate solid fuel stove in the bitterest of weathers, men tried to sleep and eat. That was, when the weather condition allowed the cook to cross the exposed foredeck with the food – there was no room or time for them to do much else. In bad weather the noise and shock of the bow slamming into the waves and the violence of the motion meant that men had to sleep jammed into their bunks as best as they could to avoid being thrown out on to the deck, which was often awash with water. Such was the motion at times that it was akin to riding a roller coaster and trying to sleep at the same time as the bow would, alternatively, climb skyward and then nosedive into the trough of a wave while, all the while, rolling viciously from side to side.

Conditions on deck were no better. The crew often worked waist deep in the icy water that poured in over the low gunwales. They toiled between the two bar-tight steel warps that ran the length of the deck when towing the trawl. These warps could slice a man in two if they parted under the strain and the ragged end slashed back across the deck. Such events were simply regarded as the hazards of a job that was full of risks.

At hauling time the skipper would call the deckhands to start the winch to reel in the warps. The warps would crack and bang under the strain and send showers of water everywhere. Huge flocks of screeching birds would appear almost from nowhere, attacking the emerging nets, straining with their load of fish. Mollymawks, kittiwakes and gannets wheeled and dived over the catch, seeking to gorge themselves before it was landed.

The trawler would have fallen beam on to the sea by the final stages of the hauling. This was when the crew brought the footrope with its line of huge, iron bobbins inboard. The crew would guide the gilson winch as it slowly lifted the footrope out of the water and clear of the rail. The cod-filled end of the net would be swung inboard to hang, dripping, over the deck. Stooping under the load of fish the mate would release the knot securing the net and allow the fish to cascade down on to the deck.

All this would happen in a heavy swell that could see the weather rail lifted ten feet above the water one minute and plunged a foot under it the next. Limbs and fingers were frequently crushed or amputated. Sleep was a rare and precious commodity snatched one or two hours at a time when fishing allowed. When on the fishing grounds, the job took priority over eating or sleeping. If the fish were plentiful and double bags occurred, the deck would not be cleared of fish before it was time to haul the gear once more and drop the next catch on the deck. Food, often just sandwiches, had to be grabbed by exhausted men as they headed for their bunks to try for a few precious hours sleep before they were shaken awake, once more, with the cry of 'hauling time'. In between hauls the crew would often be roused out to chip away the ice that was forming on the standing rigging and threatening to capsize the vessel. Or they would have to turn to and mend a torn or damaged trawl, repairing the meshes with large, wooden needles loaded with rough and abrasive manila or sisal twine. Small wonder, then, that their hands would be as tough as leather and with fingers thick and powerful. Day and night for up to three weeks the crushing routine went on and a man would have to be really injured to stop work.

It was men such as these portrayed by Alan Duggan that chiacked and joked alongside me to bring some Christmas cheer to our bleak, linoleum-floored hospital ward and help each other forget their pain and injuries. Fish and fishing were their life and their livelihood, but also their hardship and their pain and death. It had been this way since the last part of the 19th century and remained so until most of the fleet was wiped out in the devastating 'cod wars' with Iceland in the 1970s.

As a Customs officer, Dad worked in and on the docks, clambering in and out of the sturdy little trawlers in his search for contraband and mixing daily with these super tough and weather-hardened men of the sea. One of the fortunate perks of the job in those times of extreme food shortages was his ability – whether legitimately or not I do not know – to keep our house well supplied with the freshest fish, which his contacts down on the docks had taught him to skilfully skin and fillet; and which Mum served up every which way possible. The real treat was the raffia bags of scallops (known locally as tannerogans) that he regularly brought home fresh off the boats, still in their unopened shells.

Orderlies trundled trolleys down the ward, dispensing an austere but still traditional Christmas dinner to the gallantly festive patients. As I awaited my turn, a nurse arrived to whisper that I was having 'a special treat brought in by mummy and daddy'. I was puzzled more than excited: it was hard to imagine what could be more special to an eight-year-old boy recuperating in hospital during a wartime Christmas than a thin slice of turkey with cranberry sauce. The mystery was short-lived. The orderly lifted the cover off my 'special treat' – a steamed fillet of hake in white parsley sauce. Fish! Not more bloody fish! You can have too much of a good thing, even in wartime. I never forgot nor fully forgave my parents' kind but misguided thought.

Earlier that same year there had been another perceived indiscretion on the part of my parents for which I also temporarily refused to forgive them. This was the announcement of the impending arrival of another member of our family. In my juvenile mind, this was simply not on. There was no room in my world for an intruder, blood relative or not. Anecdotal history records that the closer the birth became, the more I railed against the newcomer. I protested and objected, little realising the inevitability of events proclaimed by my mother's swelling belly.

I plotted and schemed. The climax came when I explained to my parents in gory detail the fate that awaited this looming sibling. I would be taking it up to the attic – a huge, bare boarded room with a dormer window and 'secret' door into the roof space. I would lay it out on the floor and, using my carpentry set of blunt saw and even blunter chisel, hack it into little pieces before disposing of it in the big oil drums littering a nearby disused army campsite.

It must have been the shocked look on my parents' faces as they listened to my brutal scheme that caused me to soften the blow slightly. I would, I told them, put plenty of newspapers on the floor to ensure there would be no bloody trails to scrub off the wooden floor. They smiled indulgently, obviously pleased that I had heeded their early teachings to always clean up one's own mess. They smiled even more when, a few weeks later, on October 6, 1943, this same fratricidal child held his little sister's hand for the first time and beamed adoringly at her sleeping form. All thoughts of blood on the attic floor had been banished for good.

Oddly, those wartime years before and after Judith's birth are remembered mostly as a time of fun with an underlying awareness of shortages, restrictions and danger. We lived far enough away from prime targets such as London and the Midlands to miss most of the German bombing raids but were well aware of attacks on the docks in nearby Liverpool and Barrow-in-Furness and saw the occasional errant Luftwaffe plane brought down in Morecombe Bay. When this happened there was a ready trade in Perspex, which we school kids scavenged from the planes' windscreens at low tide and laboriously carved into rings and other gewgaws. We did this with the help of pokers and other implements heated until red-hot and then applied to the Perspex. The stink this caused remains in my nostrils to this day.

Barbed wire fences along the esplanade and huge cement blocks scattered on the beach to repel invasion forces were other reminders we were at war. So, too, were the concrete gun emplacement blockhouses along the foreshore and the frequent air raid warnings. Everywhere we went we took a gas mask in a cardboard box with carrying strap. Babies, such as sister Judith, had a full body mask – something akin to a humidicrib – in which they were encased whenever the sirens wailed. Windows were striped in bands of sticky tape to minimise shattering in bomb blasts. Blackouts were strictly enforced by excessively diligent air raid wardens alert to the tiniest pinprick of light showing on to the darkened streets.

It could be said we had 'a good war', living in that embattled little island yet relatively unscathed by the Battle of Britain, Dunkirk, Luftwaffe bombing raids, doodlebug versions V1 and V2 and the stringent rationing of food, clothing and essential services. Food and clothing ration coupons were carefully hoarded and sparingly spent. Basics such as eggs, milk and butter became rare luxuries, replaced for the most part by ingenious (and tasteless) substitutes such as the pallid yellow powder which, when added to water, was supposed to take the place of a farmyard egg. Carrots were used as a bakery sweetener thus leading to the creation of the cake that was then a cheap and filling staple and is now coffee-time fare for the trendy health food set – and at $4 or more for a meagre slice, if you don't mind.

Mum preserved our clothing coupons by becoming a highly competent seamstress and making nearly everything Judith and I wore, treadling away late into the night on a solid old Singer sewing machine. Likewise, Dad became a part-time cobbler, learning to sole and heel our shoes and fixing iron and rubber horseshoes on to the soles of the wooden clogs that were daily wear well beyond the confines of the local fishing community. His collection of cast iron cobbler's lasts remained with us long after the war ended and doubtless helped save the family thousands of pounds in shoe repairs. And Mum sewed, stitched and knitted almost to the very end. Neither would have understood or approved of today's disposable society.

Despite U-boats, submarines and aerial attacks – to say nothing of the natural hazards of the stormy Irish Sea – Fleetwood's fishing fleet put to sea, but not always to fish. They did duty as escorts, patrol vessels and minesweepers, as they had done in the First World War. Two boats, the *Lord Minto* and the *Arleta*, were early victims, sunk by gunfire in a submarine attack after their crews had been transferred to a third vessel, the *Nancy Hague*.

Seventeen of the port's vessels were requisitioned by the Admiralty for naval use. In the first few months of the war, seven of the fleet that had remained fishing were lost. This toll soon rose to seventeen. Fleetwood trawlers also sailed right around the British coast to help in the evacuation of Dunkirk, rescuing troops from the French beaches while under almost constant attack by enemy aircraft.

One such vessel, the 327-tonne *Evelyn Rose*, returned from a trip to the fishing grounds, landed its catch, re-provisioned and then sailed the next day to Dunkirk where it rescued 317 soldiers and ferried them home across the Channel to Ramsgate. Despite being damaged by enemy shells and bombs landing close aboard, the trawler returned to Dunkirk harbour and embarked some 400 of the British, French and North African troops that were fighting a desperate rearguard action. On the voyage back to England, 37 of the passengers were wounded by enemy aircraft fire and the vessel had to be beached at Ramsgate to allow the wounded to be taken off. The *Evelyn Rose* was the last vessel to leave Dunkirk harbour and its skipper Arthur Lewis received the OBE for the part he and his crew had played.

The war also meant the creation of the Home Guard – that poorly equipped force of earnest part-timers so well caricatured in the TV comedy series *Dad's Army*. Dad was part of that army, proudly rising to officer rank as a second lieutenant. Before each weekly muster he would rigorously polish his boots and buckles to mirror perfection, clean and oil his rifle and iron sharp creases into his rough serge tunic and trousers.

We can laugh at this band of misfits now, but at the time there was much proud parading and deadly serious intent behind their preparations to repel the enemy storming our beaches. And while we awaited this cataclysmic event, we packed our picnic baskets, filled the Thermos and covered the pebbly beaches with a blanket as we sat on sunny days and watched the tide roll in across the vast and treacherous sandbanks of Morecambe Bay.

Suddenly, it was all over. Peace was declared. With the end of the war came the next of many moves imposed upon Dad by HM Customs – to Greenock on the Clyde, to the channel port of Dover and to Southampton and its nearby airport of Eastleigh. And while he was living in "digs" all around the coast of Britain, Mum, Judith and I became somewhat reluctant lodgers in Nan and Gramp's house at 20 Charter Street.

The Charter Street house, when occupied by only my grandparents, was surprisingly spacious for what was essentially a lower middle class workman's home. But once we three had moved in it became a cramped double-storey terrace of the dreary type seen in so many British TV dramas. It contained three bedrooms up a narrow flight of stairs, a front room, central family room, a roomy kitchen, a scullery that today would be called a laundry, and a cellar. There was no bathroom or shower and the toilet was outside, between the house and a well-tended garden that produced much of the household's vegetable needs.

My little back bedroom, two steps down from the room where Mum and Judith slept, looked out over other terraces sloping down to the dockyards and the two huge gasometers rising above a waterside open space called The Strand. A washstand with china bowl and jug was my en-suite, complemented by the chamber pot under the iron bedstead.

The front room, overlooking the street, was rarely used and almost forbidden territory. An aspidistra stood in a brass pot on a wooden stand in one corner and heavy net curtains provided a screen against passers-by who might want to peer in. A low cement wall acted as a barrier between the room's bay window and the footpath, which was no more than a metre away. In this minuscule front 'yard' (really no more than a concrete strip) was a manhole, its cover lifted when the coalman called to allow him to empty sacks of the fuel into the cellar below. Black dust billowed everywhere and the musky smell seeped beneath the cellar door and into the dining room above.

As an 11-year-old boy I saw the cellar as a place of mystery, excitement and adventure, dimly lit by a single bulb and full of corners and crevices to explore. Almost airless, it smelt of a musty mix of sawdust, coal dust, the earthiness of sacks of potatoes and slightly pungent aroma of skeins of drying onions.

The shelves were full of tins and jars holding all manner of nails, screws, bolts, washers, hooks, brackets and anything else that Gramp thought might just one day turn out to be useful. Other jars and bottles contained the fruits and jams bottled by Nan and Mum to see us through the winter. All manner of tools – saws, chisels, planes, gouges, punches, hammers and pliers – were racked above a solid workbench. This was where Gramp cut, hammered, glued and screwed (in the nicest possible way) on an endless stream of household projects and repairs, including re-soling and re-heeling our shoes.

A large square heavy table, covered in a thick felt-backed embroidered tablecloth, took pride of place in the central family room, lit only by one narrow sash window looking out on to the back yard. A black leather chaise-longue filled one wall, a large sideboard another and the alcoves either side of the fireplace were taken up by glass-fronted cupboards holding the 'best' china and glassware. The furniture left little space for people. We had to squeeze our way around the table and once everyone was seated movement was almost impossible.

Three steps led down to the kitchen with its Aga-style stove providing heat for cooking and also for boiling up endless kettles and pans of water to be poured into an iron bath brought in off its hook in the yard for our weekly bath. Here Nan rested from her chores, wrapped in a floral apron and a cigarette permanently drooping from her lips. Determined to suck every last drop of nicotine, she gripped the weed between the tines of a hairpin, the better to hold it to her lips to the bitter end.

Privacy was at a premium on these bath nights, with doors from the family room and out to the scullery opened only after plenty of knocking and advance warning. Just how the adults squeezed into that bath, hardly big enough for a skinny pre-teen boy, remains a puzzle.

An Anderson shelter, every home's wartime refuge from air-raids, was removed from the back garden at 20 Charter Street and left a mess which took hours of digging and hoeing by Gramp to return to a productive veggie patch, much-needed in the time of food shortages that we as victors suffered while the enemy was sustained by the Marshall Plan and other aids to recovery.

There were street parties and gatherings all over the place. Hoarded luxury foods (such as eggs!) were brought out of hiding to boost the meagre resources of the home caterers. These were days of universal euphoria, a mass lifting of depression, the big breaths of relief of a marathoner who has endured and survived the ordeal. It also meant readjustment, settling back into old environments, previous jobs or, for many, finding their wartime endeavours were no longer needed now that the troops were coming home.

The move from Fleetwood back to Gillingham also meant more schools to add to the two already experienced up north. First it was Chaucer Street Secondary for two terms and then on by scholarship to Gillingham Grammar School, where I was the sole member of my previous school in a class where everyone else had at least a couple of buddies.

In 1947, Dad received a promotion and we moved to Thames-side Rotherhithe, on the outskirts of Gravesend where he was stationed boarding the cargo boats into Tilbury and the cross-Channel passenger boats. In the conservatory of our Marina Drive house I installed a chemistry set used for making soaps, nasty smells and minor explosives, and bred pet mice. The winter of '47 was particularly vile, especially as Britain was still suffering all manner of shortages and the transport and power systems couldn't cope with the excessive snow.

The neighbours, the Moorheads, are remembered as being considered by my parents as a friendly but odd couple. They were fanatic cyclists and insistent on using all the jargon of their breed, such as calling out 'oi' to warn of nearby vehicles, which in those petrol-scarce days were nowhere near as numerous or menacing as they are today. We too, were cyclists, making many an excursion into the nearby countryside on fruit-gathering expeditions and picnics.

At some time we acquired a car, a Riley, with leather seats, highly polished wooden dashboard and a low, sporty line. It was Dad's pride and joy, especially as he'd had an even sportier two-seat Morgan three-wheeler in his early days with Mum - and had to sell it when I came along.

Gravesend provided my first grown-up movie experiences as I was sometimes allowed to trot off on my own to one of the several cinemas in town. I clearly recall being besotted by Mario Lanza in *The Toast of New Orleans* and thus getting my first taste for operatic music, this being further heightened by hearing him sing in *The Student Prince*, even though Edmund Purdom was playing the actual role. And seared into my brain is luscious Ava Gardner in *The Barefoot Contessa*. The film dealt with emotions and situations way beyond my pubescent experiences but its scenes and the passions displayed remain etched into my memory to this day. Gravesend was also where I was expected to settle into my fourth school in less than two years – and there were more yet to come. Is it any wonder I had so much trouble socialising and making friends!

Gravesend Grammar School was down a lane on the far side of town. I was a patrol leader in the school scout troop and an increasingly mischievous pupil, inserting charcoal into inkwells, mucking about in woodwork and metalwork classes (which I hated) and disappearing to the far end of the school grounds to explore male anatomy with a couple of like-minded classmates.

It was at Gravesend Grammar that the decision was made that I should learn Latin rather than German, and that I should take the craft courses rather than another language.

These are decisions I wish my well-meaning parents had never made. From this distance it seems to show a lack of understanding of my mindset and inclinations. They assumed all boys had an interest in things practical and mechanical. But it ain't always so, as proved by the misshapen copper serviette ring from metalworking class still in my possession. They also had other hopes and desires that I was destined never to achieve. This was despite the brilliant start I had made in junior school, always topping my year and even having to endure the embarrassment of being held up as a shining example to classes a year or more ahead of me. Slowly but surely the will to concentrate and learn was sapped by the unsettling frequent changes in my school surroundings.

The final clash between parental desires and my personal wants came in an interview with the headmaster at the end of my sixth form year at Falmouth Grammar School. Dad's final posting to this historic Cornish seaport had meant I had been yet again deposited into an alienating and antagonistic atmosphere where I was expected to cope with established friendships and resistance to newcomers four weeks before the end of the school year.

After a lonesome long summer break and the elevation into the sixth form there were fresh cliques to deal with. Survival was marginally helped by an athletic prowess that installed me as the school marathon champion with performances to equal local hero Harold Tarraway who had represented England in the 1948 Olympics. Outside school, however, I found a kindred spirit in the renegade son of a local Salvation Army officer who had his own demons to fight. Together we roamed the streets in tracksuits and runners, committing minor misdemeanours – often against school property – as a way of avenging what we saw as our rejection by our peers and society in general.

Crunch time came with the end of sixth form and the obligatory three-way confrontation – I hesitate to acknowledge the parent/teacher interview label attached to it – between the headmaster, Mum and me. It was two against one as they voiced determination that the next, and only, course was to proceed to university. Any other course was unthinkable; he was thinking of the status of his school and Mum of her standing among relatives, neighbours and other parents.

To them the law, medicine, science and even teaching were the obvious career paths. This was despite the fact that I had shown minimum aptitude and even less interest in any such professions. The cataclysmic finale came when I meekly informed them that I wanted to be a journalist – an idea that had recently struck me like a lightning bolt when the teasingly flirtatious Heather, the current object of my boyish desires, revealed this was what she was going to be. And why not? I had been writing almost since I could grip a pen or pencil. I had won numerous newspaper competitions for young writers. My bedroom wall was already plastered with rejection slips from an eclectic variety of magazines. The idea of at last actually being paid for what had always been a pleasure rather than a pain had irresistible appeal.

It was if I had blurted out the worst four-letter obscenity. Never had the headmaster's severe and austere study reverberated to such a word. Two horror-struck faces glared at me. For a while I feared having to administer a double dose of CPR. But they recovered and a wordy battle resumed to which I remained totally oblivious.

During the summer break I was interviewed by the kindly Claude Berry, no relation but an erudite Cornish bard and editor of the *West Briton*. He agreed to take me on as an apprenticed journalist in a year's time if by then I could type and write shorthand.

And so, when the new academic year resumed I was enrolled at the Cornwall Technical College (my tenth and final school) in a class of three boys and twenty girls (bliss!) for a year-long commercial course covering not only shorthand and typing but also bookkeeping, commercial French and basic law – and allowing plenty of time for hockey, athletics and establishing closer ties with the opposite sex.

A year later, in July 1953, I trepidatiously trod up the ancient bare wooden stairs of the *West Briton* office in Boscawen Street, Truro, into offices of sloping, creaking knot-holed floors and musty files to begin an amazing globe-trotting life which, for more than fifty years, has financially rewarded me for doing the very thing I love above all else.

But that's another story .....

THE LAST WORD

So that's it. At least for now. There are many more byways and detours that could have been taken during this exploration of my family's past. What was once a slender sapling is now a widely spreading tree with an abundant tangle of branches extending well beyond the Welsh valleys where it was first planted. And to trace and document even some of them would have plunged me into a task without end.

By the same token, to continue going forward beyond my parents' generation would bring us into the era of the living where any attempt to continue weaving a story around a fragile frame of events rather than relate the facts could well result in dispute, argument and who knows what other tribulations.

It also brings us on to the threshold of my own journey from first to last of the seven ages of man. And with that comes the quandary faced by all biographers – how much to reveal and how much to omit? Does one admit to every lapse, indiscretion and misdemeanour committed along the way or, to avoid causing offence or upset, does one gild the lily and detour around the less savoury incidents?

As a lifetime journalist, dedicated to rooting out the facts and exposing the lies beneath, I favour the path of truth and bluntness, no matter how harsh or even hurtful this might seem. This is how it was, not how I would like it to be seen. This is who I am, not some other person I would like you to remember me as being.

Yet any attempt to record my past seventy years of wandering hither and thither would be littered with inaccuracies. It would lack specifics; be short on dates and remembered conversations. There are no diaries, hoarded notes or files of fiery correspondence and treasured billets-doux from long-gone lovers. So this person, dedicated to telling it as it is by asking who, what, when, why and how, has no such basis on which to build his own life story.

It would be a fragmented and unreliable history of encounters and incidents in an era when travel was an untrammelled pleasure; of assignments and assignations; of confrontations and conflict in a richly varied career; of deceit and even betrayal; of financial lows and romantic highs; gunpoint arrests and Iron Curtain intrigues; of infidelity and forgiveness; sporting prowess and culinary achievements; and, not least of all, the numerous affairs, brief liaisons, three marriages and several long-term relationships which, for better or for worse (as I have thrice vowed) seem to delineate me in many people's minds.

Having often bemoaned the fact that I never extracted from my now departed relatives the stories of their lives and times, it seems only right that I should at some time document at least some of my own past, regardless of how vague or faulty the memory might be.

It is food for thought ... and something upon which I need to ponder deeply before rushing into print once more. In the meantime, enjoy this one-eyed view into our ancestors' lives. May they be fondly remembered.